HISTORY   THE HOME MOVIE

OTHER BOOKS BY CRAIG RAINE

The Onion, Memory

A Martian Sends a Postcard Home

Rich

The Electrification of the Soviet Union

"1953"

Haydn and the Valve Trumpet: Literary Essays

AS EDITOR

A Choice of Kipling's Prose

Rudyard Kipling: Selected Poetry

HISTORY
THE HOME MOVIE
CRAIG RAINE

ANCHOR BOOKS
DOUBLEDAY
NEW YORK LONDON TORONTO SYDNEY AUCKLAND

AN ANCHOR BOOK
PUBLISHED BY DOUBLEDAY
a division of Bantam Doubleday Dell Publishing Group, Inc
1540 Broadway, New York, New York 10036

ANCHOR BOOKS, DOUBLEDAY, and the portrayal of an anchor
are trademarks of Doubleday, a division of Bantam Doubleday
Dell Publishing Group, Inc

History: The Home Movie was originally published in hardcover
by Doubleday in 1994

Book Design by Marysarah Quinn
Family Trees by Martie Holmer

The Library of Congress has cataloged the
Doubleday hardcover edition as follows:
Raine, Craig
History : the home movie / Craig Raine —
p   cm
1 History, Modern—20th century—Poetry   2 Raine, Craig—Family—
Poetry   3 Pasternak family—Poetry   4 Family—England—Poetry
5 Family—Russia—Poetry   I Title
PR6068 A313H57   1994
821' 914—dc20   94-16525
CIP

CONTENTS

ACKNOWLEDGMENTS

"The Queen's Own Oxfordshire Hussars," "NEP and Narkomindel," "Lenin Takes a Long Bath," "Berlin Am Zoo," "A Suitcase Full of Shit," "Asylum," "Answer the Telephone," *"Du Bist Wie Eine Jüdin,"* "Mawcarse," and "Reunion" were first published in *The New Yorker*. My thanks to Chip McGrath, Alice Quinn, and Tina Brown.

    I am deeply grateful to A. D. Nuttall, Emrys Jones, Michel Treisman, Harvey McGregor, Ann Jefferson, Robin Lane Fox, Jon Stallworthy, Bernard Richards, and Bryan Hainsworth. Ben Sonnenberg has been a good friend to *History: The Home Movie*.

Pasternak Family Tree

Leonid Pasternak *marries* Rosa Kaufmann
(1862–1945) (1867–1939)

Boris (Borya) (1890–1960)
marries
Evgenia Lourié (Zhenya) (1899–1965)
divorce, remarries 1934
Zinaida Neugaus (Zina) (1894–1966)
— child Evgeny (Zhenya) (1923–)
— child Leonid (1938–1976)

Alexander (Shura) (1893–1982)

Josephine (Zhonya) (1900–1993)
marries
Frederick Pasternak (Fedya) (1880–1975)
— children Lenchen (1927–), Karlchen (1930–)

Lydia (Lidotchka, Lida) (1902–1989)
marries
Eliot Raine

Raine Family Tree

Henry Raine (1880–1937) *marries* Queenie Ray (1881–1948)

Eliot (1904–1983) *marries* Lydia Pasternak

Norman (1911–) *marries* Olive Cheesbrough (1918–)

Alice (1907–1915)

Jimmy (1917–1970) *marries* Enid Lawrence (1915–1955)

child Lisa (1944–)

child Craig (1944–)

PROLOGUE

And me? Secret Pólice.
Third Department Cheka
NKVD MGB. KGB ETC.

An alphabet Of course.
What else but the filth
in a thousand disguises?

1905:
A Dacha by the Black Sea

Pince-nez like the letter g,
Rosa is seated, upright
at the upright piano,

letting her fingers rummage
for a few slow bars
of Brahms and Schubert

in its open drawer,
before she finds Rachmaninoff,
whose head develops

slowly, stroke by stroke,
crew-cut, severe, three-quarter face,
on the easel in the studio.

Another life in oils,
beyond this empty music stand
that little Lidotchka,

insinuated on her mother's lap,
pushes to a parallelogram
while Rosa looks for lice

"Shura! *Shu*ra! Where is Shura?"
Boris, older, is in the garden,
a bee unnoticed on his arm,

frowning at the naval squadron
far out to sea. The red flag
he's read reports about

is reading black against the sky
"Shura!" he shouts "Shura!" The name
a headache in the dark indoors

He wants the telescope,
but Shura is busy being a girl,
his cock and balls

between his legs,
reflected in the looking glass
of passe-partout and blackened mercury

And where am I?
Seeing this son from behind,
arranged like a bulldog.

And Zhonya? Where is she?
Kissing the dacha steps again,
speaking to splinters

who have suffered so much
and will suffer much more,
laying her lips along the grain.

And where am I? Forensic.
Where the turpentine broods.
By a bouquet of brushes.

Lost in the palette's latrine,
turds of fresh pigment
bright from their bolsters.

So many sticky ends.
Leonid, the painter,
wipes his hands on history

and throws it away:
crumpled columns of Cyrillic,
Gapon, banners and petition,

not a word left in line.
Then newsprint stirs and blooms,
as if the letters lived

1906:

THE VICTORIA PALACE

Buzz. Front of house, the King.
Ich Deal. Bertie Edward. Tum Tum.
Incognito on the town.

In the second dressing room,
that celebrated male impressionist
who needs no introduction

from the occiput of Africa
to the coccyx of Tierra del Fuego,
Oxford's own Miss Queenie Ray

takes a Leichner No. 7,
nips it like a *papirosa*
and adds a moustache to her 5 and 9

A tick of black. A mirror tick
She licks a brush and loads the point
with lilac to outline her lips,

reflects on her reflection,
completes the job with cochineal.
Her mouth begins to kiss itself,

then stops. She tests a smile out.
It vanishes without a trace.
Her hair is patent leather

with pomade, her patent shoes
are coaldust in the cracks,
her suit too tight for pregnancy.

Five minutes, please
Backstud, bone china dicky,
starched collar points

a pair of piggy ears
soiled slightly pink,
cufflinks, gibus, cane

She does the tipsy toff
by business with the monocle,
and hiccoughs as a facial tic

Nothing loud or broad
and far too subtle for an audience
distracted by the King

Risking her private routine
of the toff taken short,
she turns her back on everyone

Left hand on hip, she looks
both ways The right is urgent
but invisible, the elbow

barely moving Like a violinist
On their toes, the legs divide
Her head is down, but thrown back

when a cymbal simmers in the pit.
A shake A pause She bobs
her bottom out and buttons up

The audience are not amused
She dies the death
Curtains sweep the stage

"She took her Bradburys
and buggered off,"
the flyman tells stagedoor

"The only effing patter
she's effing fit for
is tiny effing feet

I nearly had a heart attack.
I could see His Majesty was shocked.
But beautiful turned out

I love them trouser creases
up the sides he wears,"
the flyman adds, two ticks before

he comes over all funny
and has to take a seat
until, too late, first aid arrives

In bed, she waits for the words:
"He was, exactly like, *her* . . .
the Widow   . Mrs Collins . .   the Bearded Lady "

1915:

THE QUEEN'S OWN OXFORDSHIRE HUSSARS

A tackroom in the trenches,
its earthen walls
whitewashed like a camembert

On his letter form he writes:
Serg 197394 Henry Raine.
My dearest Queenie,

Your news about our little Alice
came as a bit of a "blow "
Just like that Diptheoria

It makes you think.
Try not to brood about her.
I have a helmet for the boys

not a scuttle mind or what
they call a pickle howb,
its a shako Well they'll see.

Half the regiment
is to be transferred
from AT to a Cycle Corps,

but nothing certain yet.
It would have been her birthday
week after next I miss you. H

He turns the shako in his big hands,
solid as a leather motorcar
Mudguards back and front,

a radiator badge, spare wheels
holding the chinstrap double
like a bumper on the peak.

Bags of room in the boot
where it bulges to clasp
the curve of the head

A present from CENSORED.
Its beauty censored itself
by the field-cover of grey

Twenty UP saddles 1912
are gathered in a corner,
scenting like a beagle pack,

and a Hotchkiss machine gun
stares out through the slit,
propped on its elbows.

Shoecases, mess tins, bridles,
leather boots for short Lee-Enfields,
fetlock gaiters, portmouth bits,

webbing, pickets, Webley bullets
blunt as crayon stubs,
water bottles deaf with felt:

his language, this tongue,
this stable way of life
will be lost in translation,

just as the battle becomes
a pair of scissors on a map.
Instead of a chestnut

kiss-kissing up crumbs
on the palm of his hand,
a bicycle with solid tyres

So much on his mind
I miss you means that sometimes
he is stirred by the pleat

at the back of a British Warm:
they call it the Chinese chink
or Widow Twankie's twat.

Silk underwear survives
in the feel of hoarfrost
on a blade of grass:

a melting reluctance
that stiffens and stirs
and buckles with blood

As he comes with closed eyes,
he calls to mind
Instruction for Recruits:

if she'll do it, she's got it,
so when you're missing your missis,
take the wanking spanner out, lad.

Disgust. He tucks away
the tang of bloater paste
Mucous membrane of a worm

And now there's work to do.
The horses' respirators
are improvised imperfectly:

nosebags crackling with hay
like Christmas stockings,
waiting to be watered

It is better than nothing,
but only just. The mustard
burns the eyes as well,

carving out chancres,
and works on the hooves
like spit in sherbet.

With two misshapen canvas buckets,
he makes for the water-wagon
two trenches away,

as a bombardment begins:
old Bill's Jack Johnsons
and a chorus of minnies

DiphtheeeeeeeeeriA.
Under everything he hears
the voice of his daughter:

Dad, I can read in my head.
I don't say it out loud.
It's lovely. Watch.

I move my eyes on the words.
That's all that happens.
I think-read the words.

She would have been eight
the week after next. Alice.
DiphtheeeeeeeeeriA.

He risks a look,
a look at no-man's-land
A rusty can is raising

its hat The khaki dead
in Phenate-Hexane masks
are fixed, like horseflies

feeding on filth
with a black proboscis
and bulging perspex eyes.

Spilling his water,
he tacks to the tackroom,
rebandages his left puttee

and paints the horses khaki
for the dawn patrol.
A mummy with embalming blanko

1917:

Volkhonka, Moscow

A pair of throbbing woodpeckers
terrify the foggy streets
Sounds of vodka on ice

say something has begun again
A tram brakes with a yelp
in its old iron scars

and passengers disembark,
without a word, seeing
the driver drop from his cab

A dark green grasshopper,
cold in the dank daylight
at the end of Volkhonka.

A thousand kisses on your lips
Boris puts down his pen,
bored with this bogus letter,

the fifteenth today:
between the lines
space for invisible ink

Unnecessary now perhaps,
given the gunfire
popping like fat.

Caught in the chemist's shop
at Lesnoy Street, the girls
have run to cousin Fedya's flat,

panting, laughing, tearful,
fighting their skirts
and a stitch up the stairs

"Lida Zhonya Come in, come in
Sit down Let me introduce
Irina Dmitrievna, another refugee "

She smiles and lifts her coffee cup
in silence, then takes a sip
and tucks 'away her legs,

shedding a pair of Hermès shoes
The left tips on its side
"So good of Fyodor Karlovich

to take us in. So generous "
They keep their coats on
and shyly nod agreement

Fedya wedges in his monocle,
straightens his coat
and goes to telephone their parents.

"Fedya here You guessed Good
As soon as it's safe Of course
God knows Two or three days at most "

Together they try to watch
the cautious chess below,
from windows four floors up

Long motionless hours
and then a man is shot,
running, foreshortened, for cover,

clutching his bowler hat
like someone caught
by a sudden gust sideways

Firing once, his pistol skitters
across the fantailed boulevard,
followed by his hat, hesitant,

tipsy, tottering, out of true.
He is wearing white socks
and only one shoe

Wind plays with his hair
Soon there are sixteen dead
dossing in their own dry blood

and every corner is nicked
and notched like a door edge
used for measuring heights

Straightaway, electricity fails,
except for odd seconds
when the filaments glow

like someone's final drag
on a cigarette end
After three days, food is short

but Fedya's kerosene buys kasha
and a screw of salt from neighbours.
In a week, the water runs out

and Irina Dmitrievna lies
in the empty bulletproof bath,
reading Turgenev: *Smoke,*

then *Fathers and Children,*
then *A Nest of Gentlefolk,*
then *A Month in the Country.*

She is irritable for cigarettes,
complains about the cold
and the crick in her neck,

blaming the horrible draught
from the overflow pipe
Once, gripped by the giggles,

she burns Griboyedov in the stove,
all five volumes, gleefully
"You don't mind, Fyodor Karlovich."

He stands, in need of sleep,
his face somehow uncertain,
blurred by the need to shave

When shelling starts,
they move to the central stairwell
with all their neighbours·

a forest of candle stumps,
primus stoves, bedding, pans,
and Zhonya horrified to hear

the thumping of rats
only inches away,
like panic in the plaster.

She comes to prefer the bombardment
Silence brings the sound
of rifle bolts snacking like dogs

and someone trying keys
in the outside locks,
swearing placidly to himself

Lydia is too tired to care.
This is her open mouth.
This is her thick saliva

And this is a direct hit
which brings down the ceiling
and destroys the skylight.

In the dizziness of dust,
Fedya's grey ghost
folds Irina in his arms.

"O Fedya, I'm frightened."
And Zhonya understands at last.
Revolution happens in her head.

Irina Dmitrievna, another refugee,
Fyodor Karlovich, so generous,
seen as if half-naked on a bed.

Navy-blue socks, she thinks.
The milled welt of a Hermès shoe
Nothing is as it was.

She has seen someone die
Buildings have subtly changed,
pitted like snow under a tree

Even the tough bluebottle,
transmitting morse code,
can be cracked

like a chocolate
against the glass
to show its fondant centre

1917:

GARDEN SQUARE, OXFORD

The wide wooden rollers
have opened their lips an inch,
eloquent with ectoplasm

Sheets come out as cardboard,
taking their time to fold,
flannel vests like salted cod.

It is a bad back-end Nothing
dries outdoors. The clotheshorse
waits with hessian hinges

for Queenie to lay the fire.
Old *Oxford Mails* provide
a pile of paper sticks.

She moistens a corner in her mouth,
then the slack is taken up,
rattling like a blind released.

Thinking of something else,
she knots them into triangles,
her fingers black with printer's ink.

When the door-knocker bangs,
bangs, she wipes her hands
and goes upstairs to answer it.

No one there Across the road,
the garden square darkly drips,
open now, its railings requisitioned

by that Taffy get, Lloyd George.
The pavement empty either way,
she turns again to the house:

at the top of the steps,
she can see the black thread
attached to the knocker,

and senses the culprits
concealed in the night
Knocky-Nine-Doors. Kids.

She puts the lock on the snib
Soon her slippers are wet.
But the search is futile,

because now he is here,
waiting, behind the front door,
the hands in his pockets

jumping with blood His face
is clenched, his body shaken
by laughter or fear or cold.

So at first she isn't afraid
He is young and obviously ill
or sickening for something.

"What's wrong?" she asks, concerned.
Slowly his mouth tears open,
but he cannot speak He shakes

his head and shows her the razor.
A nervous moth of light
flits over the ceiling

Eliot, Norman, Alice, Jimmy:
she thinks of the children asleep,
forgetting that Alice is dead.

So when he points to the stairs,
she takes the lower flight
back down to the basement

"Is it money you want?"
She reaches the tea caddy down
from the high mantelpiece

and the gas bill behind it
drifts down to the floor.
Two views of Bridlington,

foggy now from fingerprints
He sorts out the sovereigns,
half-crowns, crowns, tanners and bobs,

sweeping the tea back in the tin
"It's not the brass ah wants.
It's thee Tek yer stuff off."

The dialect is fake and frightening
"It's cold," she counters.
"Can I light the fire first?"

He throws a box of Swan vestas,
left-handed, awkwardly.
His right hand holds the razor,

little finger crooked.
With an open page and the shovel
she blazes the kitchen fire:

sucked in the draught,
the spread of Situations Vacant
trembles like a kite

He has to rehearse in detail
every "mucky" thing she has to do,
and how many times, and where

When she knows what to say,
when all the moves are planned,
she strips to her stockings,

afraid he will be impotent
and dangerous He musn't leave her
for the kids to find in the morning

"Say use me like a toilet "
"Use me like a toilet."
"Say it." "I love you "

She tells him his story,
till he comes in her hand
with the smell of bleach

She does it like domestic chores,
making them both a cup of tea
before the shaving and the sodomy

"What do they call you?"
He thinks "My name, tha means?
You can call uz Mablethorpe "

Naked at the kitchen tap,
watching the water wash away,
clear, lenient, empty, chaste,

she turns her tired eyes
to Alice standing in the doorway,
eating a Garibaldi biscuit

and scratching her leg.
Sandals, as ever, on the wrong feet.
Then, then, she dissolves in tears

1917:

WOODSTOCK ROAD, OXFORD

A pair of sturdy steel-frame spectacles,
complete with quarter-face and nose,
designed to mask disfigurement

Adjusting the sit,
he catches a whiff of her cunt,
haunting his hands.

One startled cobalt eye
and a petrified plastic cheek
It might be Ozymandias

but it is "Mablethorpe," whistling
along the Woodstock Road, unrecognisable.
Swatting his trouser leg with *The Times*

1918:

THE ARBAT, MOSCOW

Tightly upholstered in tucks
like a boxing glove,
the chaise longue's adjustable rest

holds the weight of his shaven head.
He addresses the ceiling,
excitable, ravenous,

while Boris reflects
on the way a mouth works:
keeping out and consuming,

this versatile valve
for kissing and conversation
a sphincter restlessly red.

"When they knock their brains out,
it's like watching someone vomit
on their hands and knees,

and it sounds the same exactly.
All our plans for poetry
so much pig swill on the grass.

Eh! Just think. And their boots
bang next to your eye Dubbined,
obese, dull as liquorice.

Listen If it's winter, well,
there's a Turkish bath of steam
and they use the snow

to clean their rifle stocks.
Borya, I can't be wrong.
All day I can taste the treachery.

It's everywhere. It's in this room
She says I'm getting paranoid,
but I see it all so clearly.

Bodies Lugged like paraplegics
Lolling Trailing their heels.
And the sound of the spades,

out of puff, like a train
Did I ever do you my train?"
The great mad head turns,

greyblue, a battered ballbearing,
a question in the eyes
"No," Boris says,

although he's heard it before.
It's French, a party piece,
and consists of only one word.

Merde, like a groan, like a gasp,
like a confinement gathering speed,
running the sound into itself,

a syncopated shallow panting
of *Merde. De. Te. Merde. De-te*
Merde-de-te. Merde-de-te-merde-de-te.

He might be masturbating
He shakes on the sofa, rigid,
gripped, unable to stop.

"Susik, you're not yourself today.
It's nothing to worry about. I promise.
I promise. It's nothing."

Boris tiptoes from the room,
careful to leave the door ajar,
and goes to Katya in the kitchen

"Well?" Thick black eyebrows,
heavy breasts, low, a shred
of smoke slides up a nostril.

She puts the cigarette down
and walks deliberately towards him
until there is perhaps an inch

between his cotton shirt
and the weighted curve of her dress.
"Well, he isn't well. He's ill.

He should really see a doctor."
She takes his middle finger
in her mouth and sucks.

Merde-de-te-merde-de-te-merde.
His right hand works
the dress between her buttocks

"He'll get over it," she says.
But Boris shakes his head
"No, there's something really wrong.

He gave me this to keep,
in case they come for him.
Don't ask me who 'they' are."

He takes from his jacket
an ordinary exercise book
"It's nothing really. Notes.

For his thesis, nothing else.
Latin Elegiac Verse:
Functions of the Accusative Case."

She turns to retrieve her cigarette,
gone dead on the saucer
"So what do you propose?"

She inhales and wafts out the match.
"Treatment, Katya. Proper treatment "
She grins, but the light

in her look suddenly warps.
Finally she finds a word
that comes out a question,

"Goodbye?" He nods And then
her favourite English phrase.
"a fly in every ointment, eh?"

1919:

BACK FROM THE FRONT

Alice's Adventures in Wonderland.
The golden spine claims
Queenie and the sun

Her hands are drawn to it.
One shilling and sixpence
expressed as a fraction.

Her lips aim a long breath
and leave a line of dust
in the afternoon air,

straggling yet stationary.
It lingers like magnesium smoke.
And then the little one is shy

and suddenly under her skirt,
like old Stanhope Hicks
the Studio Photographer

Carefully, Queenie carefully
puts down the book,
as if she could see a child

poised and precious
at a fifth-floor window,
and dare not shout.

Henry. Silent, smiling, handsome,
and framed by the frame
of the sitting-room door.

"Did I give you a shock?"
She is hardly able to nod
Her eyes are open underwater

She swings up the child
and puts out her other hand,
letting her fingers

encounter his brass buttons,
the prickle of khaki,
the shape of his face

"What were you reading?"
A cut on his chin
carries a piece of toilet paper

He leafs through the story,
stops at a page of pencil marks
He shows her the scribbled nest

"Our Alice," he says,
and all her features refract
in the ripple of grief

After school, Eliot and Norman
clatter down the kitchen stairs
and into the silence

of Jimmy asleep on the sofa
and the adults absorbed
in the sight of each other.

"Well, just look who's here
You look like hypnotists, you two
Don't tell me I've grown "

"Hello, son " Eliot submits
to his father's embrace
For Norman, nothing has changed:

"Dad, is it bad manners or not
to wipe the bottle of pop
when it gets to your turn?"

Together they go to the fields.
A line of willow pollards
have ceased to be themselves,

stony as the faceless emperors
on the Sheldonian wall.
But the cricket square is pale

with care and attention,
adhesive plaster removed
The patient sightscreens

survive like polar icecaps,
and at this world's omphalos
one abandoned iron castor

"Home," he whispers to Queenie,
watching his youngest lurch
on sturdy statuesque limbs.

He spends the evening
opening cupboards and drawers,
finding the ivory napkin rings,

a set of six, like smokers' teeth,
a tea strainer's peeling chrome,
Caswell's Kid Reviver,

a tin of Huttonizing Fluid,
the *Book of Common Prayer*
worn away at the corners:

and his desire, yea,
is like to a thick tile of honey,
yet he cannot leave off,

discovering a pile of handkerchiefs
ironed like booklets,
a pair of silver sleeve links,

the metal mincing machine
with MADE IN ENGLAND
embossed on the curve of its arm,

a wooden top like a mushroom.
He plays with the carving rests,
the dachshund, the panther, the fox,

resting their lead in his hand,
he opens the meat safe
and closes its pliant zinc,

he touches the oilcloth
tacked to the pantry shelves,
smiles at the smell of Gravina.

He is saving the garden,
wisteria, lupins, red-hot pokers,
for tomorrow morning early

Tonight he squats to sample
the old sourness
that lives in the sideboard,

and finds the regimental photograph
She watches while he marks
the faces of the dead.

A trellis of Indian ink
with only ten to twenty soldiers
peering out with wary smiles.

"Enough," she says, "enough.
It's late. Time for bed.
You've made a mesh of that."

Pleased by her pun, she laughs,
and opens the curtains, left
and right, ready for morning

Upstairs, in the silence,
he has waited too long
to touch the wetness

he has wanted all day.
Desire makes him awkward
like someone in the room

and he is unable to stop her
going out to the bathroom.
He smells his armpits

like a highland dancer.
Mulligatawny, masculine, crude.
She returns in a nightdress,

her face cold and clean,
fingers finishing off her plait,
neat as a flautist.

"I left you water in the jug,"
she says. Her folded clothes
rebuff him from the bathroom chair.

The loofah's shredded wheat,
three coloured flannels
for face, foot and fanny.

In the dark, he clears his throat
like a bolt being drawn
and touches her back "Queenie?"

"I warn you, my hands are cold,"
she says, as she turns to him
And they are. And they are.

She hardly understands herself
why she hates his heart
for sounding so frantic,

like something buried alive.
She cannot tell the truth
because she cannot tell,

preferring this pretext:
"Did you do anyone else?
One of those dirty women?"

"Is that all this is?" he laughs.
" 'Course not." He wants her softness
and he cannot stop now Or now.

Lying awake, she listens,
happy to hear his snore
like a fly in the room.

"You're a good-hearted man,"
she says, and eases him over
onto his side, suddenly easy herself.

1919:
THE COMINTERN, MOSCOW

How Leonid's pencil hovers
and settles and hovers again,
until slowly the head

seeps out of the paper,
bearded, bald as an acorn,
chin strained out like a sprinter.

Touching, then taking off,
until V I Lenin is there
and there on the page,

brass-rubbed rather than drawn
And damn that decanter
which is smack in the way,

disguising, distorting
the dead Volodya Ulyanov,
a face Leonid wants to exhume

The sober three-piece suit,
the neat black boots,
the spare economical voice,

speaking impeccable German,
which spares nothing and no one.
Centrists, pacifists, social patriots:

fingers displayed to fifty delegates
from a conjuror's clenched fist,
and then the empty palm

that stands for Zimmerwald
which has "outlived its usefulness."
Lenin bangs the podium,

like a man in pursuit of a fly
Apart from Albert, alias Eberlein,
whose mandate is against,

conference applauds the motion
and a new International is born.
One abstention: Eberlein

Leonid is Chicherin's guest,
Georgi from Foreign Affairs,
but I am here on my own account,

disguised as a pencil. Why not?
Consider Trotsky, otherwise Bronstein.
Consider Comrade Stalin,

Osip Vissarionovich Dzhugashvili,
who has listened all day
without understanding a word,

who sits like a goldfish,
blowing smoke rings
and thinking (in Russian) of sex.

1919:
VICTORY V'S

A cubist quarry of parmesan cheese,
salad cream, hair tonic, arrowroot,
blunt skewers of barley sugar,

Wild Woodbines in packets of ten,
or loose in fives, sherbet fountains
fused like sticks of dynamite,

butter beans in a turtleneck sack,
a bin of pearl barley, Mansion polish,
Edinburgh rock in pastel shades,

rich tea biscuits, digestives,
custard creams, Lux soap flakes
like stamp hinges, flittering loose,

streaky bacon diced to liquorice allsorts,
a telescope of standard brass weights,
and Roland Gill reckoning up,

reweighing occasional items,
pencilling prices on greaseproof paper,
his breast pocket marked like a powder burn

On the wooden tray of fancy cakes,
a cream bun grins
like a set of false teeth:

"What can I do for this young man?"
Norman is next in the queue,
reading a list, to which he adds,

halfway through, allaying suspicion,
"And, yes, an ounce of chlorodynes."
In his bedroom, a brickyard

of khaki cornerless lozenges,
each impressed with the maker's name.
He keeps them for the chloroform.

As a way of increasing his stock,
sometimes he sells his warts
to Roland Gill, a farthing for five.

One by one, Gill counts them,
finger touching their texture:
brittle little amaretti biscuits.

Then he wipes the whole hand
with his hand, clenches his fist
and puts it in his trouser pocket.

"Now those warts are mine
because I've paid for them.
They'll be gone by tomorrow "

Acquiring more means a month
and a pin—to scratch yourself,
to make another wart bleed.

Henry is having his bath,
the tap leprous with condensation,
when Norman knocks at the door.

The coma has almost claimed him:
Henry's "Who is it?" arrives
as a buzz in the brain,

a memory emptied of meaning
from too long ago.
Between words, a silence

travelling the trek of itself,
only to reach a city of sounds
where it loses the way.

He has eaten his hoard of chlorodyne.
Henry clacks back the bolt
and floats a flannel discreetly,

masking his private parts
But the boy is beyond all that.
"Dad," he whispers, "I'm going numb "

Amazed as Alice
by how his hand has gone small
at the end of his arm,

by the giant cup and saucer
sunk in the mahogany stand.
For two days, he cannot be woken,

but "on the third day,
he rose again from the bed,"
says Eliot again, pleased with his joke.

1919:

ANTI-SEMITISM AT BABIYEGOROD

A Chinese lantern, the keepnet
calms its flicker of light
in the dark Moskvareka.

Sunset touches the tub
of simmering maggots.
The river bank is littered

with tackle at Babiyegorod,
as if some rich kulak
had fallen among thieves.

Rods, reels, scissors,
three kinds of hook,
roundbend, sproat, and limerick,

caught in a cork, arranged
like the hairs on a rambutan.
This open pocketbook of flies,

dry flies, wet flies, nymphs,
a practice page of manuscript,
the same illuminated letter

perfected in different inks.
And Shura stabbing the ground
with his penknife

because he is bored, because
they could be boys again
at the end of a day. Because.

"Let's go for a swim "
Shura's slightly buck teeth
unpeel with pleasure "Why not."

Dark water draws the line
less than half an inch
below their genitals,

rubbery, circumcised, snub,
like a boxer's broken nose,
as they wade out on tiptoe

in the shock of the cold.
Boris and Shura,
dothering like diesels

on a diet of coal dust,
arms outstretched, flapping,
the joke a duet: "Brr. Bloody Jews!"

Spent wing mayflies, hackled zulus
give off their queasy brilliance
on the unkillable earth

1920:

OXFORD THEOSOPHY

Anxious, early, overdressed,
carpet-beater frogging
on his hired coat,

spotless kid spats
mushroom-plush with kaolin,
Eliot has been asked

to take the seat in the hall
while upstairs is made ready
and chairs are arranged

The coat's bad breath
of naphthalene he fans away
with his flysheet folded twice.

PHRASES OF THE MOON (it says)
A TALK BY WILLIAM BUTLER YEATS
POET AND THINKER ADMISSION FREE

though a Benares bowl
on the card table's baize
somehow solicits a fee,

which is given to Eliot,
unasked with good evening,
as people pass to the stairs.

It seems so much the thing,
he has taken ten shillings
before he discovers the gaffe

The poet will be brief tonight,
his tonsils having been removed
quite recently, not four weeks ago,

by Dr Gogarty in Dublin O'Racular,
he quoths for two hours straight,
convincing a corner of ceiling,

his notes on a postcard,
each thought announced
with a footman's aplomb:

"And if a man return to life,
is it with the same old wart
upon his nose, the same delight

in tales of theft and murder,
or but with his many-coloured soul
like one unbroken thread?"

Waiting his turn with Yeats,
Eliot sees, angled on the mantelpiece,
the aide-memoire, and pockets it

"Lucerne," Eliot's latest work,
evokes a place he's never seen,
not even in a photograph

Hierophant of the Haemorrhoid Oil,
Yeats dons another pair of specs,
keeping the poem at arm's length.

For Eliot, it is almost sexual,
like a visit to Parson's Pleasure,
the breeze strange on his privates.

" 'Lucerne is magical in summer,
but sometimes the spell is broken—
and the world is never the same,' "

Yeats recites to the room. "No doubt,
you will think me narrow-minded,
and yet I disapprove, disapprove

of a serious concept like magic
being used in this, how shall I say,
somewhat, what, irresponsible sense."

With this, the specs are doffed.
Two tortoise-shell insects
hang from a thickening hand

Eliot has a vision of his words
like a pair of feet,
white on the grass, lost without shoes

At 10 o'clock, his girl, Yvonne,
dazzled, adoring, uncertain,
is waiting by the Bridge of Sighs

Her love is a burden
"Christ, you're like my mother, you.
He said it was good Gave me ten bob

Oh, and this, as a souvenir."
The postcard baffles them both:
"Hooping cowgh mixture for Anne."

Eliot's fingers find the flysheet
still folded in his trouser pocket.
And tear it to pieces. Single-handed.

1921:
NEP and Narkomindel

His toupee was an open book
but his pallid hands
were guarded on the desk

They gave nothing away,
not the tiniest gesture,
while his wet lips came and went,

explaining to Lydia
that there were no exit visas
for the family of Pasternak

There is nothing he can do
and, as if to illustrate,
he takes his right hand

in his left, and shifts it slowly,
like a pointer, heavy, stiff,
to a brass bell by the in-tray

He tings it carefully,
leaving his hand on the nipple
and curve of the brass

Before the clerk arrives.
"Germany, you said? Parents and sister?
Yes. Your legs are very beautiful "

She has been observing his legs
The desk is without a modesty board
A metal brace clamped to his boot

like the steel stirrup
of a bike's front brake
Surprised, she looks up

Has she heard what she heard?
The official shows her
the gap left by a canine.

"Our train is leaving tomorrow.
We must have the visas.
I was told they were ready."

The beige folder is on the desk,
unopened, left by the clerk
Again, the missing eyetooth.

"As you can see for yourself,
there is no record of your application."
A pause prolongs itself

until, almost primly,
"I must ask you to leave
People are queueing outside "

Shocked, she cannot speak.
Will she be able to walk
on her beautiful legs,

out through this ordinary door
and back into Russia for good?
Never to be abroad again?

Hammer and sickle. Forever.
Gilt on red Cloisonné. Blurred
emblem of the ampersand.

She might be the North Star,
Sarah Bernhardt herself,
making an entrance:

everyone waiting watches the door,
as if the door were God,
as if the door were a loaded gun.

Descending the five flights
of grey stone stairs,
she is stopped by a shout:

it is an old man, breathless,
with trembling sticky brown lips,
who wants her to look at his papers

"You have a kind face
They won't look at my papers.
Wrong stamp Should be a circle.

Not this what's-it triangle
They gave me the wrong one.
See So now I don't exist "

She cannot face his eyes
as he stands there in tears.
He is too old He trembles too much

She hands him her handkerchief
and then runs away
down the rest of the stairs.

At home on the Volkhonka,
they are roping the trunks
with their brass epaulettes.

"I will ask Lunacharsky.
Shush. God is good."
And Leonid unhooks the telephone,

hung in the hall,
an earwig of brass and bakelite.
"There has been a mistake."

So, next morning the visas arrive,
stabbed all over with stamps,
smashed and smeared like flies.

1922:

MUSCICAPIDUS HUMANUS (PATENT PENDING)

A caricature of the caricature
all children's bodies are,
this five-year-old boy

in the scuffed German shako
hangs his massive head
and tries to endure the day.

There is no wind And nothing moves.
Yet nothing is still The world
is glycerine in water. Warps

Thistles burn, a steady blue,
like the new New World Cooker
The horizon fumes.

"Fucking bloody bugger shite":
his brother is beside himself
because Jimmy won't be banished

but sits on the stile,
a field away, watching the gang.
Jimmy has the look of cod-liver oil

when he takes out his thumb,
clean, moist, pink, seized
by seizures of sorrow.

He is wounded, wounded
He can hardly walk
a straight line for the grief.

Now they are down in the dell,
being watched through the gorse,
Buck Watson flat on his back

with wide-open flies:
his cock is like the handle
of a Gunn & Moore cricket bat

in its red rubber sheath,
an open O tight at the tip.
Which his fingers widen

until, finally, the foreskin
crinkles around the base
of his glistening glans.

Jimmy can half hear the name
of the old Apache Indian chief,
whose moccasin mouth

he saw at the matinée,
wordlessly mouthing words,
that Saturday Queenie played piano

when Mrs. Brown had a poorly turn
What do they mean, Cochise?
And why all the laughter?

Pink as a pear drop
taken out of your mouth
to see just how much is left,

the texture has its attractions.
A tacky glaze
now tickly with flies

When he jiggles it,
expression leaves his eyes
and a grey stuff comes

out of the end onto the grass,
a tangled chain of lumps
like a Russian word

unsayable with consonants.
"When you've had a milk shake,
how do you make it stiff again?"

Buck Watson smears the sperm
with the sole of his shoe
"I think about fat people. Watch "

1922:

MAD AS A HATTER

Straight glass of best,
a bulging leather gleam
like a farmer's legging,

watched to the lips,
thin suds sucked, nebula
breathed to oblivion

"We had to kiss his boots.
But right at the end
it was anything,

set up in a chicken farm,
a thousand quid,
and half a warehouse

of Sandringham hats . . ."
just to let a tyrant
telephone the *Times*.

Henry is having a pint
with Northcliffe's "nurse":
note the lump on his eyebrow,

plump as a pullet's egg
The patient playing poker.
Strong hand Royal flush

Henry remembers ex-King Manoel,
overweight outside the Mitre,
sad, posed for the press,

an open fan of creases
at his crotch, dukes up,
his linen lapels

gripped like a kangaroo,
and wearing, *olé,*
sizzle of flashbulbs,

the *Daily Mail* hat
Tweed. "The Sandringham "
A "free copy" from Northcliffe.

Drab The mighty fallen
Henry thinks if only,
of the family fortune,

the famous Paige millions,
lost alive in Chancery
for too long to care.

"The doctors advised fresh air "
Northcliffe up on the roof:
paisley dressing gown,

pyjamas, hair, words,
all blazed in the wind.
Improving his circulation.

Cause of death: certified
as ulcerative endocarditis
by Horder and Price,

or poisoned Belgian ice cream
by Lawrence or Leonard Brown,
Northcliffe's altered ego.

"He wasn't himself at the end":
his penis had to be held,
he wouldn't touch it to pee.

Dirty. Something wrong
Café-au-lait complexion
propped in the pillows,

boasting about Napoleon's hat,
how closely it fitted Titfer
tried on at Fontainebleau

"It's all very hush":
his last memo to the *Times,*
a cracked, intoxicated tenor

delivered down the phone,
and typed, and read back,
evenly, without expression

Bitch Her Master's Voice
in duplicate, committed
to paper, to the public record:

"Why does Robbins wear
a tall hat in Fleet Street?
Tall hats should be worn

only on special occasions.
He wants to edit the *Mail*
at five thousand a year. Stop "

Malignant, carnivorous,
even as a vegetable
Utricularia prehensilis,

praying and preying
on microscopic organisms
Squeezing. A gutter press

1924:

LENIN TAKES A LONG BATH

A what? A curio, a question,
floating in the formalin
like a dried apricot,

stoned, preserved in syrup,
with five singed hairs,
part of a compote

slowly coming to life.
Cold, Shura gathers his cloak,
its falling, elegant line

broken, bunched up
by his invisible fists,
like a bat in the sling of itself.

Pepa Zbarsky, chemical engineer,
an apron beard over his apron,
observes his colleague,

the mausoleum architect,
from across the lab and smiles:
"Give up? *Pudenda*. Really.

And this thing here's a prick."
Black as a truffle,
cross section of cinder.

They turn again to Lenin,
tanning the colour of biltong,
deep in his bath of marinade:

fresh oak bark, in solution,
plus lanolin, glycerine,
cod-liver oil, in equal parts

The vascular system
still flooded with formaldehyde,
his expression is fixed:

pledges of cotton wool
fill out the eyelids,
twine keeps the jaw shut

like a system of pulleys,
in and out, nostril and septum,
up and down, behind the lips.

"I'll make a sop of him,"
Zbarsky says, in English,
ducking the head

which bobs like a ballcock:
"Shakespeare. *Richard the Third.*
Not bad for a chemist

He'll soon be permanent
Old ways work best. Evisceration.
Those pharaohs knew about meat.

Keep your aneurysm needles,
your English Swann-Morton handles
for the shape-Z blades Dyes?

Who needs eosin or saffranine?"
Zbarsky comically simpers,
pursing his mouth to the corpse

"In less than a month,
he'll be hard as bloody bakelite,
with amyl acetate to stop the moths."

Shura gathers his cloak
in both hands, holding it closed,
closed as a curtain on stage,

while Zbarsky encores in English:
"Here's fine revolution,
an we had the trick to see 't "

Shura would like to whistle a tune
as proof that Lenin is dead,
but his lips have been sealed.

1924:
AINSLEY'S BOXING BOOTH

The tomcat's long left hook
and a right and a left and a left,
but I dance out of distance,

easily, rest on the ropes,
and leave him licking
his balls like a garlic bulb.

The solar plexus of the drum
a muddy mark, a stipple,
a stain, a penalty spot,

struck by the drumstick,
by the blur of chamois leather
toffee-apple boxing glove,

collecting a crowd, twos
and threes, while the boys
warm up, jab-jabbing the air.

Old Ainsley, the "trainer,"
is chewing gum like a carp,
his tight right ear

solid as a testicle,
the breathing noisy, thick,
in his bison's broken nose.

"He reminds me, your kid, of oozit,
not the Ghost with a Hammer
in his Hand, er Jimmy Wilde,

not him, not the Rochdale Thunderbolt,
no, he's more nuggety than McAvoy,"
old Ainsley confides,

costively, with puddled eyes.
"It'll come in a minute.
Yes. Him. You know. Nonpareil.

Nonpareil Jack Dempsey
Middleweight John Kelly as was "
Enigma Variations.

Variations on an Original Theme.
Eliot listens, his face
a frown of fake attention

He takes out a Luxor
from his cigarette case.
Shagreen with silver trim,

it represents debt,
like the brocade of his waistcoat
His socks are hostages,

have been held by the laundry,
pending payment of bills.
Thank goodness for spats

A toff with esoteric tastes,
Savory's Sélection Russe
with the unusual mouthpiece,

he has come from Duke Humphrey
and a privately printed,
strictly restricted edition

of Beardsley's *Under the Hill,*
which he is copying out,
regardless of regulations,

in careful copperplate
and word for word, including
Venus and Adolphe the horse,

hot, blunt and heavy
in a damp crook of arm,
vein against vein,

whose come she collects
for a *petit déjeuner,*
sending the scribe

to the Bodleian bogs
for awkwardly angled
occasional hygienic relief.

From self-abuse to self-defence,
Eliot has come to patronise
his brother and the noble art

And Norman wins in the third,
by a knockout, deceptively
dropping his guard,

then lifting his left:
a comic crib of the way
that Eliot farts in the house,

his hand a baton raised,
von Bülow incarnate,
poised on a pause

before the music begins,
when the whiff—fooh—
is conducted allegro away.

Copycat and cat's-paw.
One flyweight opponent
laid out like a corpse.

1924:

BERLIN AM ZOO

The lowslung leopard
modelling its expensive coat
for the length of the cage,

the gorilla focusing
his nostrils like binoculars
in their direction,

the Indian elephants
without their dentures,
and Fedya captivated

by his cousin Zhonya,
who cannot make up her mind
to accept or reject

his proposal of marriage
She is almost in tears
Marriage seems so intimate.

"Here in Germany, together,
we can make a new life
All I ask is, think it over."

In the reptile house,
humidity and a muscular lizard
doing its press-ups,

poised like some Lothario
postponing an orgasm,
flame licking his lips

"Is it the difference
in age? Does it bother you?"
Fedya finds himself prompted,

conscious of seeing,
fifteen years before her birth,
the Prince of Wales at Marienbad.

She shakes her head.
Brown bewildered eyes
capture his face,

its stereoscopic ugliness:
one hooded eye, the other
clenched like palsy

on its monocle,
toast crumb moustache
above a muscular mouth.

"Do you find me ugly?"
He is thinking of Marx
on the subject of money,

its galvano-chemical power
to buy into beauty.
"You'd get used to me."

She cannot explain.
"No. You don't understand."
She wants to weep for the animals.

"It isn't that," she says,
"I don't care about looks.
Yours or anyone's. Let's have tea."

Today her period is painful.
The pubic hair is crisp,
a scab of rust, tugged

by the sanitary towel.
Indescribable, the diffidence
she feels, even to herself.

She toys with the tongs,
plays blind man's buff
with sugar cubes. Love.

Outstretched aluminium
somnambulist arms. Reaching.
She has never been properly kissed.

Loops, elastic, bleeding,
the stretch-marked moirette
of her thighs from the famine

She keeps the secret of herself,
how it is to be her.
Untouchable untouchable.

"Is it because we're cousins?"
Yards away, against the bars,
the lolling mongoloid orang-utan.

"It's good we're cousins,"
she counters, lifting her cup.
"But if I married you,

I'd be someone else.
A different kind of person."
She means to say,

if she were someone else,
she'd marry him. Too late
She will live with her words.

Like the frozen hunting horn
of Baron Karl Friedrich
Hieronymus von Munchausen

thawing out beside the fire,
after an epic silence
she speaks: "So I'd better say yes "

The poor fellow can hardly follow:
"Not unless you love me."
Her answer is incredulous:

"But I've always loved you.
Always. You're my cousin.
I couldn't marry a stranger "

Fedya produces the ring,
a d'oyley of diamonds
in a platinum setting,

and closes the box
with a cluck
like a dog catching a fly.

Kissed, she is touched
by the taste of somebody else,
someone whose beauty is plain.

1924:

A Suitcase Full of Shit

I now possess, he writes,
in forceful gothic script,
a suitcase full of shit.

Brief, a letter of reproach,
unsigned, to Hjalmar Schacht,
leaving the taste of glue

from fifty milliard marks
of postage stamps. Ten of them.
A little quilt of perforations.

The jaundiced five-watt bulb
dangles like a suicide
at the end of its flex

Otto Speck, the concierge,
tilts back his head,
producing a paunch

on the neck of his shirt.
He takes a Josephine Baker
and rogers it briskly

with a match in the rear
before lighting up
and suckling the smoke.

His face is like a snap,
viciously torn into five
or six pieces, then glued

together again any old how,
leaving his expressions
hard to determine, but hard,

in the perpetual dusk
of his caretaker's "office,"
a cupboard under the stairs.

Sixty years of cigars
have packed his nose with hair
like a meerschaum pipe.

He sits, stout as a seal,
smoking, watching, weeping,
waiting to pick up her steps

on the entrance hall stone,
or hear the clish-clash of her hand
on the lift's iron trellis.

The foreign Frau. Frau Pasternak.
With whom he has fallen in love.
Whose first name is Rosa.

Who lives on the fifth floor,
with her beautiful daughters
and that arrogant, elegant husband.

He has spent to the thought
of the buttocks under her dress,
their heavy pink, pulled apart,

white and drained, distorted
where his tufted fingers press.
Sturm und Schmalz.

"Frau Pasternak. Frau Pasternak."
Her umbrella is inside out
like a rhubarb leaf

"Let me be of assistance.
What a terrible wind."
He pirouettes the pleats

and orders them one by one
like a cashier at the bank.
Then the black elastic loop.

The ritual reminds him:
"Something. I show you."
And he drags out a suitcase,

carried away by his own conversation:
"You see. Inflation. *Notgeld,* eh
Emergency money. Inflation.

Just like mental arithmetic. Eh?
If there are 3,884 presses
printing off money 24 hours a day

at 177 separate plants (yes?)
and the inflation is running
at 2,000 per cent per day,

how many people are needed?
Answer: 50 per cent to print
what the other 50 have to spend

Ha ha. Big joke, Frau Pasternak.
Big joke Something. I show you
Inflation. A fuck for six eggs."

Only aware he is urgent,
she fails to understand
even the drift of what he says.

The locks on the suitcase
flip up under his thumbs,
revealing a fortune in notes,

brick after brick after brick,
printed on Bielefeld silk
to the value of billions.

Wertlosgeld. With the one word
each bundle is identically marked.
"Worthless, Frau Pasternak,

and I just can't throw it away."
He is crying openly now,
weeping like a wedge of lemon.

"Silk, best silk, Frau Pasternak.
Like ladies' lingerie," he chokes,
plunging into the suitcase,

demolished *Notgeld,* brick after brick,
"top-quality Bielefeld drawers.
From first of December, purely platonic "

As a spider tiptoes,
quickly she tiptoes away.
Upstairs, she explains to Leonid

that "Speck is having a breakdown.
Ugh. Those beastly sabre scars.
Purple and ridgy. Like worms."

1925:

THE GENERAL KILLS HIMSELF

Every breath, a chair scraped back
across a concrete floor.
Every breath, the screek of a shovel

in cinders, grating the grate.
Every difficult breath
a shirt torn up for bandages

And when he breathes out,
the click of cartilage
throwing a switch,

and the wisp of a whistle
heard on a crystal set,
the frequency fading.

The General is calmer now.
He keeps a level head,
balanced, between both hands.

As he always does Chin up.
Like a chap being shaved
by a barber, held by the doze,

which accounts for the nickname,
except that, this evening,
blood has picked out

the detail of knuckle and nails,
like schoolchildren bent
over inkwells, busy with pens.

Norman has run for the doctor,
Jimmy is up in his bedroom,
clipped on the ear and ordered

to "buzz off this minute"
because the General is here,
incontinent with blood.

He has cut his throat
with a bone-handled kitchen knife
right through the trachea,

only to then change his mind
and dash from door to door,
his head in his hands,

till somebody came Queenie.
"Musha misha juggler."
He gargles his words

"Don't talk. Norman, get Dr. Wade."
He sits on her kitchen chair,
bleeding and swallowing blood,

his breath a deliberate slur
like the slur of the whetstone
he used to sharpen the knife.

Through the blind blinking wound,
the windpipe at work.
Now you see it, now you don't.

It comes and goes
like a glove puppet,
swallowing, swallowing

Dr Wade is matter-of-fact,
talking and sewing
while the ambulance waits,

the horse like a surgeon
masked by its nosebag.
"Emergency repairs," he says,

"a stitch in time,"
pulling the stitch
to a pimple of white

before he proceeds to the next.
He whistles a tune.
He tugs and snips.

"You missed the jugular vein.
It's a home" snip "tracheotomy.
Stick to the Gas Board, eh?"

Another tug. Another snip
Another snatch of *Rigoletto*.
The General was out of tune

1926:

A SHORT STRETCH OF NOTHING

Streaked, freaked, spattered, dribbled,
the henhouse hardens
like a painter's studio.

Jimmy Raine's harem of hens,
pluck-plucking at banjos:
c'est la vie bohème.

A bottle of Empire sherry
wears its tipsy wig
of candle grease askew.

He is absorbed in himself,
pressing his prick
like a spring

back into his body.
Whoops, it buckles
sideways and he begins again

until it dwindles
to a second bellybutton.
Quickened, it slowly

extrudes, foreskin crinkled
like the unforced crown
of rhubarb shoots

With concentrated, moving lips,
he masturbates left-handed
while he reads *Film Fun,*

his mind on Harold Lloyd,
Mack Swain and Fatty Arbuckle,
completely innocent of sex,

even though Colin Dunn
has seen the Doctor's Book
at home, bound in brown paper

on the highest shelf,
and knows the greasy band
you wear to make a baby.

And so this numbness,
like cocaine at the dentist's,
comes as a nasty surprise

His cock is there
as a short stretch of nothing
for maybe a minute,

before it jumps like a frog
in his hand, for plié
after plié, after plié After plié.

The glaring bantams disapprove.
A row of ginger musquash coats
with padded shoulders

The cock in plus fours
like Henry his father
Jimmy fastens his flies.

1926:
RONIGER

The full moon is a mother
feeding her child
with parted lips.

Nervous as a compass needle,
seven months out of Sofia
but still on their way,

they bicker in whispers
across the Austrian border
to Wien and Comrade Koralov,

Georgi Dimitrov, Party HQ,
the *Rabotnischeski Vestnik*.
It is a two day walk

through glass-paper snow
for fifteen adults, six children,
and the motherless baby

in Roniger's arms
that everyone wishes to kill
in case troops are nearby

The bumpy, clenched face
goes off like a siren,
unstopped by his hand

or his crooked little finger
worked between indignant,
trembling gums

It is a two day trek
through the Neusiedler marshes
from Fertöd to Pamhagen,

with plenty of time to see
the scenery define itself
at dawn like painted flats,

with time to remember
how Orange Guards boarded
the Tirnovo train at Dolní Dabnik

and tore out the beards
of Malinov and Todorov
and other "bourgeois traitors,"

how IMRO beheaded Stamboliski
after they hacked off his hands
for signing the Nish Convention,

how Masha once took him in hand
with a solemn joke,
"This is what we doctors call

the hardening of the arteries,"
how he came like a gong,
again and again. Her hips

were thin, flat, curved
as Roniger's hip flask.
Which, inspired, he uses now

to quell the child with kümmel,
so Kochev folds the knife away
and grins his grin of solid steel.

A few kilometres on, the baby
smells sharply of shit; then,
a kilometre more, of nothing.

A crowd of fifty thousand saw
the sacristan, Zadgorski, hang
for planting ecrasite

in Sveta Nedelya Cathedral.
Topped by an earringed gypsy,
with Koev and Marko Fridman.

Roniger was there, to report
the details back to Moscow,
not the way the bodies pirouetted

counterclockwise, then reversed,
nor how the hangman held his nose
when poor Zadgorski shat himself.

Supposing they were stopped,
what would Roniger say,
asked to identify himself?

The truth? Or lies? Or both?
Pretend to be a Bulgar,
the only definite article?

Or one of the Soviet Red Cross
sent to help repatriate
the thirty thousand Whites

disarmed by Stamboliski
and stranded in Bulgaria?
Or one of Wrangel's Whites?

Or a Bolshevik perhaps,
seconded to the party in Sofia,
but after the bomb

at old Georgiev's funeral,
a refugee from Tsankov's terror .   .
It all depends. Who asks?

He has come a long way,
almost too far to care,
avoiding the Yugoslav border

as obvious and, so, unsafe,
taking the Iskâr instead
down to the Danube.

Feinting east, then going west.
Against the current. Good
Dunai, the Dunav, Dunărea,

Duna, Dunaj, the Donau:
you can bet on the Danube,
like Roniger, to change

To change, to adapt, to survive.
It is snowing lint again,
like going blind

then waking in a hospital.
The exhausted children
are hungry and quietly crying

Roniger lip-reads a mother
telling her staring child,
stupid with cold, eight years old,

he should have died at birth.
The bridge of her nose
is wrinkled like a dog's.

Roniger regrets his skis,
their locust bindings lost,
the ski sticks propped

in the corner of that inn
and left deliberately
like a ballerina on her points.

Children. He couldn't care less.
A burden. He tightens his grip.
A risk And yet he reconstructs

his route by the children.
Children bathing in the Iskâr,
wet and naked on the bank,

cold as grasshoppers.
A toddler's tiny prick
au poivre with sand.

Right at the beginning,
in Drehovica, that girl
arranging coins, carefully,

by colour and size,
one brass, one alloy,
alternate, in a patch of sun

to make them shine.
At Sip Canal, a blond boy
learning sums, his left hand

a laborious trill of counting,
the green tablecloth
askew with concentration.

Another child at Maglavit,
who raised and lowered
a bucket over his head,

testing the altered notes
of the scale he was singing.
And Natasha's son at Buda,

addressed by a policeman
in Magyar, there on the street
The boy stood his ground

smiling a lion tamer's smile
before he went on his way,
relieved, with a ruffled head

Feelings? Feelings have left
his feet and fingers.
His features are frozen.

The kids are brilliant alibis,
protective colour
and nothing more to Roniger.

This landscape is like a film
before it starts· bright
and blank, except

for a flickering thread
like a hair in the gate
of a cinematograph camera.

When he almost expects
to start seeing numbers,
a sign appears for Pamhagen.

Only twenty kilometres more.
He tightens on his talisman
and walks. A sign. Of all things.

And the village policeman,
holding his heavy revolver,
clean-shaven, nervous, tongue

trying his cold sore, a boa
of breath coming and going,
as he struggles

to free the safety catch.
So they surrender, like children,
who want to be carried,

lifting their arms,
everyone, except for Roniger.
Then they pick up their bundles.

The inn is like a cuckoo clock
with a cuckoo clock inside it,
and the innkeeper's wife

is taking the baby,
like a cache of explosive,
crooning and crooning

As she uncovers its face,
Roniger registers
the shock of seeing far, far,

far into the human ear:
a flower's fine mist of hairs
and a stamen of dark gold wax,

which move him to tears,
carried away by what he has carried.
His arms are locked.

Lost in a last embrace
with no one at all.
He cannot even take his jacket off.

Kochev couldn't give a fuck
Grunting, wordless, he reads
the day before yesterday's paper.

Then. "Roniger, listen to this.
According to this, it says
that Tsankov has fallen

And Liaptchev has formed
a democratic government
Shit We could all go back

and use the Labour Party
as a front " Roniger sobs.
"So what's so funny, eh?"

Roniger tries to wipe his eyes
"Nothing Just that joke
about the fat Bavarian

who finds a fly in his soup
He eats it, right, and orders more.
This time, though, no fly

He calls the waiter and complains:
Herr Ober, wo ist's Krebsl? Get it?
I mean, we've come a long way

to get away from Professor Tsankov.
A bit of me, just a bit of me,
would like that bastard still in power "

1926:

THE FLY-BUTTON MACHINE

Ominous outside the forge,
this quarter-hammer loads
the table-top like gravity,

weighing its word,
its vow, a cocktail shaker
cast in solid steel,

left there by Andrew Crawford,
who heads for the bar
and turns his back on everyone,

the big blacksmith's striker,
his waistcoat buckle titchy,
glinting, like a lucky charm.

Unperturbed, Tip Musgrave tells
the one about Lunqvist
on Bank Top Station

to all the avid eyes around,
unbuttoning his shirt
in readiness, and slithering

his broad bright yellow braces
off, with a hiss,
like someone, like anyone,

like Stanley Baldwin getting ready
for bed: "The same whirr-whirr
that happened with the other chap.

But, whirr, instead of ecstasy,
this agonizing pain
In the end of his dick.

The thing had sewn a button on "
They have listened
like men waiting to sneeze.

And now their heads jerk back,
dental patients,
teeth black with fillings.

"A florin wasted,"
Tip murmurs to his signet ring,
facetiously frowning at fate.

Two tiny nipples ripen
in the body hair espaliered
up his midriff and across his chest

"If you don't mind, gentlemen,
I'll keep my hair shirt on,"
he says, and nods at Norman,

who is holding the money,
"Call Crawford over, would you?"
He stands unobstructed, legs apart,

hands clenched in his pockets,
and sets his stomach muscles
jutting like a bank vault door

Round-shouldered as an ox,
Crawford weighs the hammer, weighs,
takes two preparatory taps,

and then the hammer bounces
Musgrave totters back
Two steps, three steps Stops

"Blow me down Life after death.
I thank you, Mr Crawford.
The money, Norman. Thaaankyoh "

1928:
HAIR SHIRT

The primus in chains
like a futurist Andromeda
with a padlock handbag.

The brass fuel cap,
sited in grit, weeping
like a cracked nipple

Thin saucepans, scoured
the colour of cobwebs.
Worn lino A communal kitchen,

where a bluebottle goes mad
in the light switch
and the light bulb squints.

"In your honour, poet."
On the woollen palm
of her fingerless glove,

Maria Judina holds out
an ordinary lemon
like a declaration of love.

Not an old lemon,
with dark, thin peel
tough as oilcloth,

but a thing anointed:
beeswax burnish and blur,
bearing a twig.

Her teeth are bad,
ivory mended with mortar,
but she is beautiful

and Boris has heard
she wears a hair shirt
Grazing her nipples.

"Just as well Mother is dead
Her knowledge of kitchens
was hazy Wasn't it, Mother?

Don't look so surprised:
she's there by the window,
pulling a face. Aren't you?

Can't bear criticism even now.
When we came here first,
there was a kitchen range.

Before the primus stoves.
She opened the oven and said
she knew what it was for

Didn't you, Mother?
For burning wood, she said.
You burn wood in here "

Voice a sudden husk,
her gaze a glitter.
The hand, though, is steady,

fingers meting out lapsang,
a trickle of black
straight into teacups,

like withered nails,
an archaeologist's find.
They rust and storm

in the boiling water.
A wheel window
floats in each cup.

"Servants saw to everything,
you see Shall I play?
Alexander Nicolayevich?"

The piano fills her room,
her bedding underneath,
Scriabin open on the rest

"Look at the notes.
Scriabin's Sea of Galilee,
clear as a snapshot,

and Christ in the left hand,
still half asleep,
composing and calming the waves."

She wrings her cold hands,
looks up from her lap,
begins, as if the keyboard

had her by the wrists
And in the afterwards,
in the deliberate silence

which prolongs itself,
his hand is taken, squeezed.
They press past the piano:

"I want to show you something.
Voilà! A poet's moon.
Describe it for me "

The full moon prompts,
but he is lost for words,
unable to perform,

until he remembers
a simile seen by his son
from different curtains:

"A brightness, bruised,
like the face of a radish."
He wants to laugh.

"My son's idea, actually
He's only five Zhenya
His mother was making a salad.

He saw it and showed me.
On the wet chopping board,
a tiny coin of radish "

The child's sad face,
its brightness also bruised,
making the word: moon

And Maria's sad face now,
saying, "A clever boy. Sure
And handsome, eh? Like his father."

The tea still on her breath
Tar. Her compliment hurts.
"Not exactly, no," he says,

"he suffers from freckles."
Thickly blotted with bran
on his cheeks and nose

Boris has complained to Leonid,
pages of purple ink,
that they "will ruin his life,"

and been answered with banter.
He cannot be candid,
but he cannot keep silent.

A few freckles Are nothing
Footling. Unless they show
his son is not his son.

He cannot look this fear
full in the face. Which face?
That face of brightness

bruised by distaste
which is badly disguised
And the fear is founded

on nothing: only a conscience
queasy with lust, like now
"I would like to kiss you."

"Of course," she answers,
this hair-shirted saint.
Of course she answers of course.

Inverted nipples. Empty circles.
Pink as chiropodist's felt
for cushioning corns. Perfect.

And the shirt? A string vest
Henequen knotted by hand
Did he expect a garment from GUM?

1929:

Locum Tenens

Bugs and drugs behind him,
scraped through somehow
at the third attempt,

almost pukka Harley Street
in his short black jacket,
pearl grey waistcoat,

grey herringbone trousers,
Eliot is *locum tenens*
at Virginia Water, practising

at general practice,
and just about scraping through
with less than a week to go

Something flat on its back,
dead on the windowsill,
arms folded like Pharaoh

Phlox and photosynthesis,
a brilliant day,
but his lips are a line

Dread. He is frightened
to touch the telephone,
foetal, trailing its cord,

a cry on the desk.
Has it come to term,
the threatened pregnancy?

"Virginia Water three two .   ."
Listens Oh hell It has
Except for that once

as a student observer,
he's never actually in fact
But when he did his clinical

he passed the gynie
And even through fear
he thinks, a second chance

to see a woman's Oh hell
The district midwife
has prepared the area

Her safety razor
has bitten off more
than it can chew

It gags in the basin
Below the rash of hot splashes
on the big bald pubic bone,

a fresh gash, engorged,
overripe, alluvial,
the inner labia

like chicken livers,
the segmented anus inside
out, a blood orange

"Her waters have broke,"
says the midwife's mouth,
one tooth tinged with lipstick,

"presentation's normal,
if you'd like to check
Soon be over now."

The presentation isn't normal.
When Eliot feels,
it feels occipito-posterior

and therefore trapped
Or perhaps. But then
The midwife must know:

the confident crackle
of her rubber gloves
like hot fat, the click

of her starched cuffs
on the dresser, the play
of her muscular forearm

making a sweep, dusted
lengths of terracotta-coloured
rubber piping "Push."

Nature takes its course.
He comes and sees her,
he goes away, he comes again.

"There now, here's Doctor."
He tries Pituitrin
to advance the labour,

injecting the air
with a fly-fisher's cast,
and then her taut vagina.

Little sobs of bright blood
at the point of the needle.
A brilliant day:

people are playing tennis,
badly, on a, nearby, court
like bradycardia

He comes again, he reassures
the husband in the kitchen,
avoiding his eye,

aware of the tap's elastic drop
held in suspense,
butter beans in steep,

bursting their condoms
He leaves   After 24 hours,
she is too tired to push

On the pillow, wet hair,
lips the colour of cement
Eliot calls in the partner

Occipito-posterior
Too late to. Save the mother.
Episiotomy   Both hands

whiten on scissors
Forceps and fingers.
Somehow the foetus

unfolds   Like a telephone
Eliot answers an arm   Dead.
He wishes he'd never been born,

and asks the partner afterwards:
"Will I be struck off for this?"
"Good God, man." And, kindly meant,

"It's only a baby. No.
She can soon have some more."
Now he can afford to feel

for the worn-out face
like a Victorian penny,
suffered, utterly spent,

a ghost which has seen a ghost,
forever vague,
the mind's veronica.

1929:

ONE FOOT IN THE GRAVE

Soft slither of excrements
as she trims the surplus pastry,
dish rotated on her hand

Egg, bacon and potato pie:
chevron snipped into the top,
brushed with beaten egg and milk.

Queenie, at the kitchen sink,
whittles, lips pursed, brisk,
shavings of raw dough

from her clogged red fingers.
And I am rubbing my hands,
my hands and my head:

an affliction like dermatitis,
the desire to be clean
The tap is in tears

Henry runs the pastry rowel
back and forth. A wheelbarrow.
He is trying to speak.

But. There is a difficulty
A pain in the sinus
dissolving the words.

There is an obstacle:
love he feels as furniture,
as a three-seater sofa

stuck in the stairwell,
its hessian underside on show,
its castors comically prim

"Is it the boy?" she asks.
He nods. Her image drowns.
"The limp?" He nods again.

"And he's shown you?" He nods
"And?" And Henry shakes his head.
"You'd best bring him down."

So Norman sits, eighteen, blank,
with his bags rolled up
like some Masonic ceremony.

His left leg, for no reason,
has shrunk to stone,
a glazed length

of rock salt, warped,
red and ready to weep.
He will never box again.

"You should have said,"
she says, bent down to look,
so he can see her parting

then the parting of her breasts.
"Yes. It needs the oil. A film.
I'll go to Hancock's."

Over the chemist's counter,
the formula for linmethsal,
kept in the Bible, preserved

on a plain postcard. Judicious,
Charlie Hancock like an umpire
deliberating his decision.

"I'll make it up this afternoon":
a green ribbed bottle
tight in brown paper,

filled with compound liniment
of methyl salicylate,
eucalyptus, olive oil,

tight as an onion, carried
through the rain, past blowpipe
tphs of burning leaves

and stumbling paraplegic smoke.
In the dark kitchen,
the reek uncorked, she works

the warmth into his leg:
thick whisky taken, taken,
till her palms are coals.

Will I wear a cripple boot?
Norman wants to ask,
but cannot speak his mind.

Instead, a focused fear,
full of blunt detail:
he can count the laceholes,

he can see the leather,
lengthened by dread
like a hall of mirrors,

sheer as the sides of a ship
At the back of his brain,
he practises, tries out

the tiring weight
and the toppling walk.
He gets in training.

The kiss of the cork replaced
and then the other business
with the spool of film

exposed deliberately
to what is left of the light,
then burned like a flypaper

coiled on the kitchen coals
with whatever was caught.
"This leg will live," she says,

"I won't let you lose this leg."
Kicking her old high music-hall kick,
for emphasis, perhaps

1930:

ANIMAL MAGNETISM

Listen, listen to the water
washing in the gravel pit
like a little girl

wearing her mother's shoes
The wind at Wiesbaden
finds the wet cusp

of Misha Kroll's eyelid,
exposed by his monocle,
the colour of cooked ham

He is wearing nothing else,
being proud of his penis
and about to take the plunge:

white feet walking the plunk,
plunk, plink of the planks,
toneless warp of the wood.

Flaps like a beechnut,
his Russian fur hat
weighs on his German clothes.

Naked, no one would know
that he was Stalin's doctor,
or that he'd overseen

the softening of Lenin's brain.
At forty, trim as a boxer,
Uncle Misha in the buff,

part of Lenin's legacy,
the brain surgeon, bathing
before a breakfast of eggs

at Haus Dambachtal,
the small hotel his sister runs.
Like a pair of pliers

a frog flips into space
from the end of the stage.
Uncle Misha is more cautious,

inches down gymnastically,
lowering his legs, slow
as someone paralysed,

then side-strokes away,
his monocle mercury
in the morning light.

At night, he entertains
by hypnotising women guests:
a risqué business

of lifted dresses, garters,
stocking-tops and laughter.
His sister disapproves:

a former pupil of Frau Pasternak,
she prefers the piano,
a light salad of tunes

from Offenbach and Strauss.
Misha lowers the tone.
But Natasha, his niece,

who still remembers Russia,
regards him with awe,
with awe and affection:

he finds her attractive,
and when she recalls
how the firemen's water froze

on the floral carpets
so the children could slide
when the fire was finally out,

Uncle Misha listens,
as once he listened long ago,
avuncular, professional,

to the donkey blare
of her whooping cough.
He lets her light his cigar

Together they take the train
(tickets tucked in his hatband,
the beechnut in his baggage)

to Berlin, to her parents,
to the Pasternaks (for tea),
to all of Wagner's *Ring*

where the girl is hypnotised
and held by the harnesses
holding the Rhine-maidens aloft,

in which she sees suspended
the survival of her brother
in the TB sanatorium,

his leather corset
correcting a spinal curvature.
She grows into another life.

1930:

SEQUESTRA

Zhenya switches his front tooth,
hypnotic, woggly, on
and off. On and off,

while his mother, Zhenya,
is cracking cob nuts
between her teeth, doggedly,

with the one-sided grin
of a six-year-old learning
to wink The kernels pile up

But Boris cannot look at them.
At the rust on the nuts,
frail as dirt from a fingernail

Or Zhenya, or Zhenya: the names
a claustrophobic throb
like the generator downstairs.

Boris has toothache,
toothache like the moon,
her introverted look

of swollen suffering,
his heart in his mouth,
beating and aching.

It all began the day
of Mayakovsky's suicide.
Spring Outside the windows,

a single magpie perched,
back to the breeze,
its tail turned up

like the corner of rug
beside the iron bed
The big body lay

under a navy-blue blanket,
all but the head invisible,
and that was turned away

where the hair was shaved,
a faint blue bruising
like a hard-boiled egg

Boris was trying to cry
when the sister's voice
climbed up the stairs

clumsily, indignant, arguing
every step of the way,
and entered the room

completely alone,
with her brother's face,
the mouth, the hands, the eyebrows,

and crying out, "Volodya"
Seeing the corpse,
she stopped her mouth

and every feature spoke
instead, suddenly slurred,
as if they were drunk.

She sat on the bed
and stared up at the ceiling,
silent, smoking, destroyed,

waiting for her face
to heal enough to say hello.
But when the cigarettes

ran out, she gathered up
the stubs, and left,
unrecognisable, without a word.

There was a quotation
from "The Cloud in Trousers,"
something quite appropriate

but unsayable for Boris
whose lower lip was dead
and felt exactly like felt

A symptom of something,
he thought at the time
but quickly forgot,

being entranced
by the caretaker's entrance,
by the chisel in his boot,

used to chip out putty
from the winter window frames,
which he carried out

on tiptoe, awkwardly,
back and forth,
till every casement opened.

Suppurative osteomyelitis
leaves the taste
of pig shit in your mouth,

loosens the teeth,
infects the mandible.
And has to be treated.

Boris sits at the table
and lets the hump of the loaf
summon the dentist again,

neckless as a fly,
his antiseptic hands
holding the buzz,

his scalpel, his chisel,
and the chip on his shoulder
and the chip in your mouth,

chipping off the dead bone
until the healthy bone
sweats pinpricks of blood

and the patient faints
Then the periosteum
is sutured back in place.

The casement hangs
on its hinges. The buzz
of the drill is stopped.

And the ache will not end.
His mouth must be cleansed.
He needs fresh air.

Was it ever real,
his love for Mayakovsky?
Or just a rivalry disguised?

The table stretcher
is worn down to a yoke
by the family's feet.

The boy lounges
between his mother's legs
like a cello

She tousles his hair
What plucked at his heart
now throbs in his gums.

She gets on his nerves.
He will get a divorce
Have Zina in Kiev Throb.

1930:

THE FINAL PROBLEM

Glimpse. Visible from Row A,
the welts of her stockings
pulled into widow's peaks

by sturdy suspenders:
Lady Conan Doyle, in black,
takes the tragic stage,

one dizzy Jacob's ladder
just above the knee.
Something to look up to.

Norman is sunk in the depths
of his front-row seat
for the best possible view.

Queenie prods her son
with the programme. Slovenly.
Show a little. Over and out.

A crowded Albert Hall,
ten thousand in the audience,
full house for Conan Doyle

six days deceased in Sussex
George Craze Esq. presides,
his hearing aid

like a lost spermatozoon
having a word in his ear.
To womb do I undress myself?

A single empty chair
is set aside, centre stage:
Sir Arthur's seat

Will we hear its wicker?
Feeding falsetto gasps,
creaky as a newborn baby?

Is Albert in his consort hall?
Is it one of his haunts?
Victoria, before she died,

her hair like a hen
settled and brooding,
would hold his miniature up

to any interesting sight
he might otherwise miss,
being dead to the world

Will Albert come through instead?
Ask Mrs. Roberts,
the unhappy medium,

hot in her fox furs,
who removes all her rings
and addresses the chair,

announcing Sir Arthur is here.
"But only in spirit,"
Norman whispers to Queenie

In the café afterwards,
they quarrel A bandstand
of tiered fancy cakes

is left untouched.
She is furious He, facetious,
staring through the strainer

like a magnifying glass:
"Elementary, old bean
Wish-fulfilment, Watson.

Like Holmes's comeback
after the Reichenbach bout.
Alive by popular demand."

And on the train to Oxford:
"Moriarty's name was James.
Two brothers. One a colonel,

also by the name of James.
The other was a stationmaster
Just thought you'd like to know."

His mother is silent.
He has gone too far
and can only go further:

he would like to make peace,
but out of the ether,
singing, his voice is heard,

"Pearly gates. Pork and beans.
Good old pork and beans."
To the tune of "Jingle Bells "

From Reading to Oxford,
all the way, unable to stop.
Pearly gates Pork and beans.

And in the garden later,
he cannot let it rest:
"Or this bee in rugger kit

White shorts Reincarnation.
Conan Doyle turns out for Guy's
Or did he play for Bart's?"

Angry with himself,
he makes a mark with his heel,
and buries the bee in the lawn

Home for the weekend,
almost absently Eliot intervenes:
"Actually, it was Edinburgh."

1931:

SIDESHOW

Jimmy is up in the cradle,
selecting a suitable writer:
an extra-small swan,

sable with Kolinsky filling,
or, better, maybe a goose
to flood in the dipper

He prefers a point to a chisel
Tasting the chalk line still:
unwaxed linen thread, sourness

snapped between his lips,
leaving guidelines of dust
where the letters will go.

He has the spacing in his head
In his hand, greatness,
laid on the mahlstick

which flattens its muslin nose
like a miniature pudding
tied up for steaming

With five years to go
before he is out of his time,
this apprentice at fourteen

can signwrite a sign
better than his boss at fifty:
Tillotson of Tillotson & Son,

stout, ambling, stooped,
nervous of heights,
one afflicted watery eye,

the pores of his nose
pinked by port and lemon,
a baggy polar bear in overalls.

Cold. It is January
Words are white in the air
as puffs from a pounce-bag

The skewered rides
are packed away for winter,
for the annual exile:

crowned heads incognito,
all their regalia
stowed under canvas.

The tattooed lady
keeps inside her caravan,
or, shopping, covers up

her skin, floral Axminster
under long kid gloves
like an arm in plaster

The bearded lady shaves
Without drawing the curtains,
so that Jimmy has studied

the slap of her breasts,
weighed up their whiteness
swaying like cheese wrings

when she whisks the soap
in her Ladysmith and Mafeking
Commemoration shaving mug.

A pair of reserves
for the Boneless Wonder,
whose sign is Jimmy's job.

The nipples are vague,
without an aureole,
two tenacious drips

of the palest pink whey.
One letter left to do
when Tillotson whispers:

"Churchill. Fuck me pink
with a blue stick of rhubarb."
The lad is so surprised

he makes a slip on the *r*.
"Always wipe mistakes
back into the letter, boy."

He reaches for his rag
as Churchill's voice
reaches his ears.

Those squelchy consonants,
confident and carrying:
"They were never out of black,

Brendan, the Victorians.
My nurse, I remember, poor thing:
her relatives died like flies."

Bracken and Churchill
taking a turn to Battersea,
arm in arm, after sitting all night.

Burly, bowler-hatted,
breathing brandy hard,
Churchill reads the sign aloud,

over tortoise-shell glasses
pulled to the end of his nose
And laughs. Laughs and leaves

Turps on the rag Wisps
A small snow falls
like freshly grated parmesan

Later, in the afternoon,
Churchill addresses the House,
disputing the Bill for Trade Disputes:

"What does the Prime Minister
propose to do if defeated again?
The other day I spoke about

his talent for taking tumbles
without any visible hurt
He falls, but up he comes again,

dishevelled, discommoded,
yet always smiling
And I remember, as a child,

being taken, many years ago,
to Barnum's Circus by my nurse
Among the many freaks,

the star attraction,
which I most desired to see,
was billed as the Boneless Wonder.

I pleaded with my nurse,
but urged to no avail.
Another time, she said,

when I was a bigger boy,
for now the spectacle
would shock the system

and demoralise my youthful self.
I have waited in vain
for another time to come,

without ever giving up,
and after sixty years
my patience is rewarded.

These eyes rest at last"—
he points to the Treasury Bench
—"on the Boneless Wonder."

Bracken, writing to Randolph:
"We're back from the dead.
The Boneless Wonder is immortal."

1931:

TURNCOAT

Words clearing his throat,
lips ajar and out of sync,
jowls sprawling, blood-silted,

on his frayed shirt collar,
"Pecs" O'Hanlon gives advice,
bronchitic as a bulldog:

"Like pulling purse strings
Lugs is trouble for a fighter
Best to lance the ligature and   ."

Quick, his open hand contracts
into a fist,
as if he'd snatched a fly.

"Turn the record over, Pecs
You're getting on my wick
I've got a broken nose already.

Don't sell me a cauliflower ear
because I'm not buying it. O K ?
I want to look the way I look."

Norman's hair is vaselined,
waterproofed like astrakhan,
a shining example.

He massages his right ear,
carefully, with hot milk,
as hot as he can bear

Attentively, the mirror
chained above the mantelpiece
tilts towards him.

A word in his ear:
bruised, it says, bruised
like a bloody black pudding.

The captious cockerel,
a landlady's man himself,
gives vent in the garden

Mrs. Fulton's other pet,
a big black velvet tom
with a threadbare nose

is out for the count
on her travelling rug,
a reversing MacDonald sett

with alternating colour
in the overcheck. G B. C
Blackwatch, the dog-eared cat.

His split-pea eyes alert,
he bats a ball of string
machine-wound to a turban.

Every evening, entertainment
Records on her Cliftophone.
Norman's nifty quickstep,

Elsie Fulton in his arms,
flirtatious, over forty,
full-figured, solid

as a tailor's dummy
It couldn't be more innocent:
chaperoned by Mr Fulton,

his melancholy photograph
watching from the mantelpiece,
chaperoned by Pecs,

who winds the box,
folds out its prolix pincer,
and sets Victor Sylvester

hissing, dizzy, on the baize;
also chaperoned
by Elsie Fulton's bosom,

braced between them,
single, abstract, chaste,
unyielding as a bolster

"If you were the only girl
in the world and I was the only boy,"
it couldn't be more innocent,

until she falls,
trying out a fishtail turn
Too late, she claws her dress.

Knowledge They have read
her homemade muslin pants:
Lyle and Tate and Ly

The record sizzles to a stop.
Out of register,
like a tuppenny blood,

her thin smile betrays
the lavish lipstick
of her cupid's bow. Mercy

Ease the pain. Nothing drastic
"Turn it over, Pecs.
Blackwatch, time to go outside."

1931:
ASYLUM

The pock of a pipe removed
by the male sister in charge
and then his smoker's smile

of creosote, tartar, plaque
A cyst on his cheek
threaded with blood,

he points out the patients,
names and conditions,
while Eliot follows

the bitten bakelite stem
on its intricate journey,
the mouthpiece

an oracular pout
of miniature ebony lips
like an African sculpture:

"That's Cheops Robinson
You only ever see him
sideways on Fucking crackers.

For he's a jolly good pharaoh
You have to laugh.
How-do, Cheops? Eh?"

In the chronic male ward,
iron high-sided cots,
mesh on the high windows,

three horizontal ropes
securing horsehair mattresses
which line the walls,

and, at night,
a dull port-wine stain
at the end of the ward,

like a blotch on the retina,
which is only the stove,
clenching, unclenching its red

Treatment is standard,
secure, behind the times,
nothing occult,

containment, not cure:
paraldehyde and lukewarm baths.
"Applied economics,

you might just say," he says,
kissing his pipestem,
little kisses, keeping it on,

"soaking the rich,
soaking the poor. See?
Restores mental balance."

Men who are women,
watched by male nurses
in rubber lace-up ankle boots

and dark green rubber aprons,
full-length, a quarter-inch thick,
solid as a capsicum,

making movement ungainly
They could be slaughtermen,
strength in their folded arms,

untouched by the touched
and their tone-deaf noise:
the bleats and the lowing

that live in these throats
They angle their heads
strangely, listening, vacant,

to what is within,
whatever it is which seems
so angry and so sad

"They come here, some of them,
with less meat on them
than a jockey's whip

Now look at them: pregnant,
double-breasted to a man
Must be the potty meat Eh?"

When Eliot fails to laugh,
the male sister chuckles
and elaborates "Cream crackers

Brazil nuts Bisto crazy
See him? That one, there
With the periscope up

He used to be scrum-half
for Pontypridd and Wales
Evans Wife trouble

Before he came here,
capped for Wales he was
Fly-half. Poor bugger "

Hairless, heavy, soft,
Evans is troubled by sex,
his sudden hardness

which is hypnotic
for the nude, forgetful mad,
who gather and, gathering,

lose the thread. Of what.
Or why Do not disperse,
docile at their destination.

Not unlike Eliot,
who has answered an ad
in the *Lancet*. Successfully.

The only applicant
for Assistant Medical Officer
at Derby County Mental Hospital

inspects a safety smock,
kept in case of mutiny,
"if anyone goes really bats."

Tested for weight,
it tinkles with buckles
like a tambourine.

Four afternoons a week,
Eliot takes the bus
to change his book

at Boots in Derby,
watching the lambs startle
on dirty pipe-cleaner legs,

and one night, towards teatime,
returns to find a charge nurse
lugging Evans from the lake.

Drenched and dead Eyes open.
Feet bare Sousing
stabs of water Sabres.

"It's only three feet deep.
Impossible to drown yourself
He misbehaved deliberately.

Couldn't have done it
without the safety smock.
Salvation, in a way

He'd had a bash before
Wife trouble. This way, see,
he couldn't help himself "

After supper in his room,
Eliot writes to Mapother,
begging a post at the Maudsley:

"I see no future here."
Trailing canvas wings
which cross and buckle behind

like a pipistrelle
tying itself in knots,
wrapping things up

1932:

FRENCH FOREIGN LESION

On the unmade iron bed,
a tattered *Petit Vingtième,*
open at the opening episode

of "Tintin au Pays des Soviets"
by Gabritschevsky's friend,
inscribed "à Yenia, grâce à lui,"

and signed "Hergé (Georges Remi)."
The pomegranate head,
Norfolk jacket and plus fours.

The last sardine of lunch:
a crinkling transfer
of molten tin. Tinned.

The lid like a mainspring.
At one end, a tilted
wedge of olive oil

he uses to anoint her lips.
Yenia seems a different person,
somehow not himself today,

a sign around his neck
that says DO NOT DISTURB,
explaining madness

as a psychological sestina,
a tinnitus of thought
like Siegfried's ostinato anvil

and the tintinnabulation,
four pianos and percussion,
of Stravinsky's *Svadba.*

"Les Noces, it's called.
Bauernhochzeit The Wedding
Will you sleep with me?

I suppose I needn't say
there's no one here I want "
His eyes assume an idiot vacancy.

"You like me, don't you, Lydia?
Maybe not so much as Yura,
but I'm better in bed

than little brother Really
Lots of practice. Before all this.
How? With prostitutes, of course

I picked them up in Munich,
outside a little purse shop
Königsallee, near the station

Open late. Quite smart.
You bought a purse inside
and if they took it, then you knew "

She thinks of Hoch,
financier and Fedya's friend,
favoured by her parents:

the way he offers apricots,
suede lockets, softness
pressed between his fingers,

the way his fingers
feel like gloves,
his breathing bluish lips,

his false ivory teeth,
clenched on a torn cheroot
like a flapping cuff.

A close shave, Hoch.
Shuddering, she suggests a walk.
And now she licks her lips.

Sardines. Sex. Of course.
Sex is the something strange
she has already sensed,

felt like a word
on the tip of her tongue,
insistently absent

like Yenia's moustache,
removed by a nervous barber
deputising for "Herr Dienstag,"

who comes on Tuesdays
from his premises in Schwaben,
but who this week was ill.

No one here can shave himself.
She says, "I'll think it over.
Now, put some shoes on, please."

Yenia Gabritschevsky,
exile in exile,
with Saturday stubble,

may leave the grounds
with suitable companions.
Securely, as instructed,

Lydia links their arms,
like lovers almost: only,
she could break his wrist.

Gentleman and gentle man,
artist, sadist, dipterist,
he did his doctorate

on the screwworm fly,
which insinuates its eggs
in wounds or any orifice,

both animal and human
"My thesis advocated
breeding sterile males.

If I ask her nicely,
think she'll suck me off?"
Up the trail towards them,

a frowning girl
follows her arms, bent
as if by the breasts

in her Bavarian blouse,
blond wickerwork hair
slick at the temples

Lydia has her answer ready
"Sssh, on no account
You haven't even shaved."

"Weisse Scheisse," he says.
"You're right. I always forget.
Most improper." His gaze

unsteadies, quickens, spills.
Tiny stuttering steps
take them to the valley floor.

And so she agrees to sex,
on Saturdays, for six months,
in his private room

which lacks a lock.
The china doorknob wedged
by Yenia's bentwood chair.

Hot, half-dressed, oral,
anal, painful, prolonged,
for pity's sake.

Inserting barley sugar
in her cunt, he whispers
"Fräulein Sonnabend" and comes. At last.

1932:
BY APPOINTMENT

Whitewashed coal aches
in the sun along the wharf
"I name this ship the *Challenger*.

May God preserve her
and all who sail in her   ."
At the perforated line

of portholes, heavy, clamped,
faces like bottled fruit.
The hand-picked crew

Edward, Prince of Wales,
in uniform at Portsmouth,
is doing his duty.

He lifts one hornet sleeve
and the green skittle
of vintage Bollinger,

a muzzled magnum
with a golden hilt,
smacks against the bows

Brief cauliflower.
Cheers Rivets like mangetout.
What a hoot Cheers

And now David must dash
to cut a dash tonight
(discreetly, of course)

with Wallis and Ernest
at the Duce's new drama
somewhere in St Martin's Lane

He can change on his train,
get details from his diary:
Napoleon: The Hundred Days

by Benito Mussolini
and Giovacchino Forzano.
New Theatre (TEM 3878)

He arrives after 9, late,
and enters the perfumed box
Wallis, ironclad in odour

He has missed the worst
of Robert Atkins' bombast
from the north cliff of Elba

Napoleon's second time around
is nearly over. Fouché
instructs Real in realpolitik:

"Gratitude? In politics,
there is no such thing"
Soon this Minister of Police

manipulates the deputies
until the elder statesmen,
Jay and Lafayette, demand

the Emperor's abdication.
The critic of the *Times*
already feels for phrases:

"history lies quietly open;
the comment of the Fates;
the audience continuously held "

In the dark, David finds
and fondles Mrs Simpson's knee
Vigilant shuteye for Ernest.

Almost nodding off at 2,
Eliot writes up his diary:
"Two tickets for *Napoleon*,

three shillings each.
Supper at the Trattoria Verde,
five shillings each

Let me touch her breasts
in the taxi Nothing more
No gratitude at all.

Says husband home from sea
Large investment. No return
Returned to Maudsley."

After breast of guineafowl,
mangetout "like a battleship,"
and quick spinet laughter,

David does embroidery
"My secret vice," he says
Fine surgical stitches,

her eyebrows are attentive,
her crêpe de Chine pleated
like celery Slender Hard

The cotton membrane is pricked,
taut as the cellophane circle
on a jar of preserves

1932:

SUICIDE

The phone is hysterical,
holding its hands
over its ears Screaming.

Zhenya scratching her face.
Wild cornered eyes
trapped in her head.

Snot in her hair,
on the back of her hand
trying to tear

too many pages at once
of his new book, *Second Birth,*
then roughly smoothing

them out, leaving them
bent She was suicidal
He couldn't lift a hand.

Now, from the other room, Zina:
"You answer it. I'm playing
mahjong and she isn't my wife."

Someone is eating his words.
Can you hear? There.
Soft mastications,

vowels swallowed. Drunk.
"Who is it?" Boris asks,
and hears small, separate

sounds of satisfaction
A child quenching its thirst.
Sex Or someone dying Then,

dazing the metal diaphragm:
"Alleluia, alleluia,
Alliluyeva's shot herself."

A buzz of ohms Click
He lets the telephone fall
and brush the carpet

like the arm of an ape.
He feels sorry for her,
for Stalin, for himself.

He has already thought of this
Fear has imagined the details,
has made up her mind:

the chip off her tooth
where the sight
was sharp on the barrel,

the rancid taste of oil,
the weighting altered,
tiring her wrists,

hard to hold steady
She took her own life
while its balance

was disturbed. Thumbs
pressed to the trigger
So stiff. Then *exeunt omnes.*

A slogan of blood
daubing the tiles,
ceiling, light bulb, W C

It might have been Zhenya
But when Fadeyev brings
the letter of condolence

for the *Literaturnaya,*
already bearing signatures
of thirty prominent writers,

Boris refuses to sign
It is too sycophantic
Soviet Socialist grief.

Zina is beside herself:
"Your name will be missed.
Sign. Everyone signs "

Boris sips a glass of tea.
"Fadeyev is fond of me
And I never said why "

Zina will not come to bed.
She sits playing patience,
keeps a lighted cigarette

between them, her anger
always vigilant. Untouchable.
Unfaltering Separate Stone

"They know what it means.
You say you sympathise.
Then sign. Or go back to her."

The erotic smack of cards,
insolent slap after slap
in the face, until he writes:

"I share my comrades' feelings.
As a poet, I was there,
seeing and suffering everything."

His right hand writes
the truth in purple ink.
His left hand is lost

in his hair, philandering,
sending down showers. See.
Drifts, inside and outside.

1933:

DIE VIEHBREMSE

Just a jug in its hairnet.
Alma mater. Plain white china
on the windowsill of 12:13.

Eliot shakes a leg into the leg
of his haunted trousers,
hired only this morning

Eliot is German learning,
therefore in the accent thinks.
Thinks that Rilke story,

reciting and rapt
How did it go again?
He stares at his studs.

"Grossmutters Kleid
hast du getragen,
mit weissen Rosen

und Ärmeln gepufft
Dein Kleid
aus Grossmutters Tagen.

In den Falten
liegt noch der Duft "
Something like that

And the fake falsetto
of Kraus, the Viennese gadfly,
mincing his words:

"Grossvaters Hosen
hast du getragen   . "
Rilke crushed him with a look.

Eliot crushes his reflection,
his double-ended black bow tie
tweezed and tweaked,

plucked and palped
to a pair of sculls
neat at the neck

Will Norman remember?
I need your black shoes
Features slightly unfocused,

a vaseline blur, listening,
out of breath, to his brother
Earless. The leather head

solid as a soldier ant,
cased like a cockroach
in his abdominal shield.˙

A bib of sweat. The gloves
great amber beads on the rope.
An idiot's abacus   The old one-two

Eliot, in shirtsleeves, paces
the room on staircase 12,
restless as a referee

The college Visitor crosses
the quad, episcopal gaiters
cracked like a hen's

Seven strikes Fellows gather
under the great fig tree.
Fruit cup sways

in its silver bowl
as two college servants
carry it into hall.

Eliot watches from his window.
There's that fruit Jenkins
Being brilliant, blast him,

with every bone in his body
Then Eliot has his idea:
black socks over brown shoes,

brave face and bugger Norman
Later, passing the port,
circumcising a cigar,

Eliot expands and expounds:
"Die Forschungsanstalt
für Psychiatrie at Munich"

(ja, enjoying the German)
"a year doing genetic research.
Rockefeller Foundation funding.

An awfully exciting field."
He postulates new animals,
biological patents, pedigrees,

bringing back the unicorn,
degeneracy, genetic hygiene,
ideas of the Übermensch

Clever, modest, considered,
he crosses his legs,
engulfed in an armchair,

and notices, out on a limb,
that one of his shoes
has shed its black sock.

"A little demonstration
of the new genetic science?"
Jenkins asks to general derision

The pillion passenger
on Norman's belt-driven,
clutchless E W Douglas

is a Somerville girl
Ada Beauchamp, an eton-cropped
Bollinger Bolshevist

They've left a ballot box
outside the Oxford Union,
full of white feathers.

Norman wears his jacket
back to front, jokes
about kangaroo petrol,

and begs her to curb
her Marxist leanings
when they take a right turn.

Over a pint she explains.
She can sympathise
with Einstein's four percenters.

She isn't like a college blood
But there will be a war.
Against the Fascists,

not for King and Country.
He is wondering why
his exhaust-valve lifter sticks,

whether she believes
in free love, what her tits
are like, will the condom keep on?

\

1934:
No Monkey Business

Seventeen, eighteen, nineteen.
Frau Alias is counting the hairs
in her silverbacked brush,

whose twined initials
cling and copulate,
while Eliot and Yeats

are doing a barn dance,
politely trying to pass
in Eugen Steinach's office door

Location. Vienna Above his labs,
fifty-eight, fifty-nine, sixty
Hauptallee, next to the Prater.

It is her daily ritual
because she believes
she is going gradually bald

Broad black giddyap reins
stream from the poet's pince-nez
during the Gentlemen's Excuse Me

Entschuldigen Sie, bitte sehr,
dieser Marmeladenverkehr, says Eliot,
before suddenly seeing

Or should I say, he says,
"the struggle of the fly in marmalade"?
Celebrity casts a cold eye

and grandly is gone. At once
replaced by Herr Professor Steinach,
whose Harley Street disciple,

author of *Rejuvenation,* Norman Haire,
has recommended Eliot And vice versa
Steinach: perspiring, perfumed,

impatient, emphatic, expository,
vigorous, voluble, Latinate
as Caesar's *Gallic War,* Book 7.

(Sixty-one, sixty-two, sixty-three
Herr Alias is laying down the law,
telling his wife she must come.)

The testicle, Eliot learns,
consists of seminiferous tubules,
whence the semen,

and also polyhedral Leydig cells,
present interstitially,
whence the hormone. Good?

The secret of rejuvenation   .
(Getting a rise out of W B Yeast,
thinks Eliot) the secret of rejuvenation

is proliferation of the hormone.
By one of two quite simple methods.
No monkey business, eh?

(Steinach permits himself
a smile at poor, pitiful Voronoff.)
One: the homoplastic treatment:

grafts on another testicle
in the area of the groin.
The site is scarified,

lightly, with a needle.
The cut surface of the testicle
is laid against the muscle fibres

and the edge of its protective sheath
sewn in place with silk or catgut
Twelve days absolute rest

If it "takes," more hormone.
Like taking on some extra labour
First performed by Lespinasse. 1911.

Two: the autoplastic method,
whereby the Leydig cells
are stimulated further

by the tubules having been tied off
A redirected labour force. Yes?
First performed Uppsala, '94

(Three, thinks Eliot, bore them rigid
His features, quelling a yawn,
seem curiously close to a climax.)

Autosuggestion having to be avoided,
early operations all took place
in the course of other ops,

without the patients
having given their consent.
Friend Lichtenstern, genito-urinary

The interview is over.
On the stairs, Eliot encounters
a couple, Herr Alias and Frau,

who quarrel in whispers.
He will give her consent
in less than an hour.

And her legs will open to electrodes,
experience their shock,
cold as an earring clasp.

She will give a little scream
and watch the trembling
of the rosewood box,

trapped, as it were,
on the Riesenrad,
between panic and pleasure,

for five or six minutes,
before the professor pronounces
her orgasm achieved.

Choosing his words: this inability,
this incompetence in intercourse,
this clitoral dependency,

amounts to this:
an insult to the penis.
Which will never be forgiven.

1934:

CONTINUOUS PERFORMANCE

Listening and tilted towards
the clear, quiet evidence
and helter-skelter ringlets

of Irina Alexandrovna Yousoupoff,
Princess of Russia, are:
the Honourable Mr. Justice Avory,

in shaggy ink-cap,
Sir Patrick Hastings K.C.,
appearing for the plaintiff

in crewcut kite-tailed cauliflower,
and Henry Raine, a juror,
bald as a blackbird's nest.

Hundred per cent horsehair wigs,
hand-woven, all bobbins and bows,
by Northams, High Street, Oxford;

make-up by Love, Interest and Libel;
sparks by politely cross examination,
conducted "with all due respect .   ."

Listening and tilted towards
the Prince Yousoupoff,
now resident at rue Guttenberg,

Boulogne-sur-Seine, Paris,
and (perhaps) Prince Chegodieff
in *Rasputin, The Mad Monk* by MGM:

"How did we murder him?
With cyanide. No, not sodium
Potassium. Cyanide of potassium.

White crystals pulverised to talc
by Lazovert. *Quoi?* A doctor. In the army.
Pestle and mortar, grinding its teeth

I remember his hands. Coldblooded
Bloodless From the rubber gloves.
Beige. Like a waxwork "

Almost his English is perfect.
The accent *is:* eating his words
like caramel toffees, chewing

the diphthongs. Of course.
As a scout, Henry remembers,
in Univ lodge at twilight,

that pas de deux of hands.
That japanned hair like modern art
Down without a degree Staircase 9

Before the war. Opening his vowels,
asking his scout to wind up the goldfish—
an eighteen-carat hunter kept in water

"Three almond cakes. Three chocolate.
Under the icing That is correct
And in the wines Madeira. Sauterne,

a Château de Rayne-Vigneau it was,
to mask the cyanide Of almonds,
my lord. Bitter, and quite pronounced

Not Archduke Constantine's Yquem,
but, still, I agree: a perfect waste.
And I don't mean *pourriture noble,* what?

Where was I? Yes. The Starets came.
Grigori Efimovich, down the cellar steps
With a rustle of cockroaches.

The sound of my own blood.
And I could just make out my voice—
offering the unpoisoned biscuits

I felt he felt, when our eyes met,
the scald of knowledge in my own.
And all he did was smile.

Have a seat, I said. I will, he said.
The wickerwork mewed like a kitten.
Silence, then upstairs

the others, the others started
with the gramophone "Yankee Doodle."
Again and again. Hysterical.

Like someone washing their hands.
Or laughing. Or sobbing. Inconsolable
Compulsive. The ancient mariner.

He held me with his glittering eye,
drank off the poisoned glass
and ate two cakes. And lived:

he drooped; he did not die;
he wanted me to play guitar.
As well as "Yankee Doodle." Aie.

Someone failing to find the spot,
that's what I was like
Left a bit. Down a bit No

Itching the chords, seeking,
scratching for Scarlatti,
fretting the frets.

Left a bit. Down a bit Yes
I could see his chin, yes,
descend like a violinist

Then came the slow movements
of his breath. It was half past two.
I went upstairs to get a gun

Cards on the green card table,
as if they were sitting an exam
They seemed not like ones who'd failed,

but like ones who had succeeded
only in arranging for an aegrotat "
The allusion lost on everyone,

including Henry, who is out of sorts,
as if (acid asides inside)
he's eaten something disputatious

"When the others heard the shot,
someone, in the rush to help,
brushed up against the switch.

Strange Darkness wasn't dark
I couldn't see, but I was seeing red "
Henry nods; agrees; comes back

"An eyelid moved His left.
Then nothing moved. I couldn't tell.
It wasn't like a lizard,

when we distinguish states
of stillness and arrest You know?
I bent down to take a closer look

and felt his fist tighten.
I screamed and left my epaulette
behind. Uprooted. Broken threads.

Like a gardener clutching a clod,
weeding a flowerbed,
the Starets knelt a moment.

No, I admit that I was terrified.
The wound? Yes, it was visible.
He wore a white silk blouse.

Less than you might think.
I'd say more like the mark
left by the new ball

on a pair of flannels.
Well, we locked him in
and he broke down the door.

Finally? Purishkevich shot him.
Out in the snow. Several times.
A press? A loaded stick.

I used one on the Starets' head.
Unrecognisable? No. Disreputable.
As if he'd been in a drunken brawl.

Bundled in a blue velvet curtain.
Dropped into the Neva from a bridge
Which one? I couldn't say

I wasn't there. I stayed behind.
To remove all traces of the murder.
Camphor on the bloodstains

Outside, oil paint tinted like the flags
Blood analysis? Of course
A single shot behind the ear for Scout

The name I gave the chow we had.
A beauty. Black tongue. Springy cinnamon
like yarn A party-squeaker tail

Coiled. What we Russians call
stepmothers' tongues A pedigree:
Hsuan Tsung, Emperor of Tweeddale

We called him Scout."
Henry, unlike the Prince, is untouched
by this veterinarian tenderness

Feeling ebbs from his finger-ends
They look as dead as candle grease,
the colour of a marble font.

Call Mrs Elise Mary Budd of Brighton,
film-goer and unprofessional Russophile,
who will testify she thought:

Chegodieff was Yousoupoff.
And that, therefore, therefore,
therefore Princess Chegodieff

(seduced by Grishka Rasputin
before she marries Chegodieff
in the final thrilling reel)

was in real life the Princess Yousoupoff.
Which is a costly libel,
priced at five and twenty thousand pound,

owing to the plaintiff's social eminence,
as argued by Sir Patrick Hastings:
"If a Mr. Smith of Balham

is arrested by mistake tonight,
the news might rate a minor notice
and his damages be small.

But if Sir William Jowitt . . ."
Laughter in court.
Jowitt is the silk for MGM.

Henry, feeling poorly, reflects:
beauty and good luggage
always carry the day.

Ironical The mockery
This successful libel suit
was instigated by a murderer.

Laughter in court.
But not in the imperial court.
Grigori Efimovich Rasputin:

pedigree: saviour of the Caesarevitch,
friend of Badmaev the Tibetan lama,
mesmerist, faith healer, Khlyst.

Henry contemplates his headgear,
lined with silk like a coffin,
where the soul survives:

the tiniest
black barathea butterfly
balanced on the leather headband.

1934:

STANDARD BREAD

A ceremonial progress,
acclaimed and heckled,
through the body of the hall,

like a steady icebreaker
creating this splinter of arms,
salutes that swell and subside

From up on the ceiling
(where else?) Olympia presents
Sir Oswald Mosley,

a home perm of seats,
and the pong of hydrogen sulphide
from the Communist stink bombs.

Sir Oswald is a damn good egg.
Or else. A blackshirt bouncer
adjusts and tightens a touch

the knot of Jimmy's red tie,
draws on his fag *(ecco,*
as a chef acclaims a dish

by kissing off his fingertips)
then fumigates
the tie's contaminated colour.

Suspect, from his aisle seat,
Jimmy affects an interest
in the woman sitting next to him.

The wealth of her flanks
redistributed, with the sound
of intaken breath,

Jimmy observes the nub
of her left front suspender,
swells, salutes, thank God subsides.

The house lights, too, are lowered.
Poised to speak at the lectern,
in a test tube of light,

Mosley lingers for silence
in silence, only to hear
the barracking begin.

A blinkered spot sweeps,
blazes like a compass card
of splintered light,

and settles the trouble
there at southeast by south,
by bringing the blackshirts

like a swarm of flies to shit.
North-northwest East by south.
East by north Southwest by west.

An hour's delay for ejections
like sandhoppers into Hammersmith Road.
Then the trouble dies down.

"We are grateful," Mosley begins,
"to those few people
who have been interrupting.

They show the pressing need
to protect free speech
by a proper Fascist Defence Force."

The woman at Jimmy's elbow
starts to scream and thrash.
It is an epileptic fit,

but the steward smacks her face,
forehand, backhand, forehand,
till her nose begins to bleed.

Helps her out by the tits.
Throwing her handbag after.
It is sick on the pavement.

A Barclays chequebook. Scent.
A charm bracelet. Lipstick.
An opened envelope.

Then the exit closes
as the blackshirt brings
its iron bar banging down.

And afterwards, some comrades
infiltrate the lectern area
and sway the podium itself

Later still, a cheeky figure
in the girders of the roof
whistles the Internationale

and brings Sir Oswald to a stop.
Ankles crossed, he asks,
before he disappears:

"Are you the same Mosley
who thought up Standard Bread?"
A climbing steward comes unstuck

Jimmy sees all this
and doesn't see all this,
since what he sees

is what he watched
as if it were a tennis match
Forehand, backhand, forehand

In Bombay, in Calcutta,
in Rangoon, in Penang, in Batavia
All points of the compass Jim

1934:

ANSWER THE TELEPHONE

Stella and Stella's new breasts
are taking their weekly bath,
monitored by Stella's family.

The full, adoring complement:
perspiring Papa, proud Mama,
little sister, little brother,

and big brother are watching
the delicate, blunt beauty
of her breasts, nipples

like dregs of rosé,
deliciously inaccessible.
Each aureole pricked out.

When the communal telephone rings
in the hall's camera obscura.
For Boris Leonidovich

Who is fetched and finds himself
staring at Stella's wet breasts
through a pinhole in the plaster

and talking to Comrade Stalin
Swung gleam (What?) Each tit
tipped like a billiard cue

) with pink morocco plush.
They hold their audience.
What? He stares up the wall,

away from the hairy hole,
at Papa's portrait of Tolstoy,
old L. N in his linen *rubashka*

like a German dentist,
hung high in the darkness
And what does Borya feel?

Power Most of all, power.
Peter the Great, pulling out
teeth, teeth by the sackful

His own begin to ache,
steadily, like testicles
after hours of foreplay

And in himself? Power, too,
importance, panic Pride and fear
Excitement almost sexual

He has the sense
that everything is clear,
intimate, but upside down

When Stalin mentions Mandelstam,
Boris feels, profoundly feels
there must be some mistake.

Is Mandelstam a genius?
(Osip Emilyevich? *Mandelstam?*
But what about me?)

Disappointed, downcast, genuine,
Boris addresses the question:
a good writer, yes A *genius* . . .

His voice trails off.
Trails off, he suddenly thinks,
like drops of blood

and sees them there,
splintered on the parquet floor,
as he sees the question,

at last, for what it is
Political. And therefore:
Osip Emilyevich is a poet

and a poet who will live
as long as Russian poetry.
Against the sentence of death,

pronounces this short sentence
He will forget the exact words
because (for him) they are untrue.

He will remember only the truth.
The things he thought.
The sense of being chosen.

The shameful sense of eagerness,
of having said too much.
Of unrequited love.

Hello? Hello? Hello? Hello?
Outside, the full moon hangs up
her radical mastectomy.

Epileptic by the geyser,
a fly, unable, injured
on its trampoline. Poised,

the doctor's black bag
hesitates, then hurries to help,
with eight horrible handles

1935:
DRAW THAT FUSE

Henry, hunched in the park,
unable to lift his head, seeing
only the broad-swung scythe

of a woman's tweed skirts
and the red-brick base
of the bandstand's cast-iron crown.

The weight of his head
deep sunk on his chest,
though his eyes are alert

to the tiny stars
crushed in the asphalt.
Lips slurred in saliva

like someone asleep
Like Alderman Horace Dainty,
"elder and lifelong member"

of the Wesley Memorial Church,
"who sleeps at peace
in the arms of the Father,"

commemorated by this iron stereotype
above the lead-tagged fuse box,
where Jimmy tries to learn

his boss's son about electric:
"electric can't be heard,
it can't be seen, it can't be smelt.

You don't know if it's there.
So if you play with it,
for badness or a joke,

watch out there's something
sharp and prickly in the wires,
that jumps out up your arm "

Little Billy, four years old,
plugs in his thumb. Learned
His father, Tallentyre,

reaches in his hessian tool sling
spread like a lake, and rummages,
then extends his fists:

"Right on, then, choose
We can't get on till electric's off
I've give Matt Newby

price of two pints
to look the other way Pick "
And Jimmy picks the paper twist

of half-inch nails, so loses.
Even with the Electric's foreman
squared, he is reluctant

"Draw that fuse," says Tallentyre,
"or get your cards "
Jimmy draws the fuse

A sword sheathed in his arm,
the alternating current
throws him right across the church,

backwards, like film
ripped out of a projector.
Laughing, Tallentyre wipes his eyes:

"The Keystone Kops. Hell,
you should've seen yourself.
Who's that nigger? Jesse Owens "

John Cleveland Owens, actually,
Ohio State, I fuss for the record,
long jump, broad jump, take your pick

The stopcock fixed, flood contained,
it's Tallentyre's turn,
since Jimmy has refused the fuse.

"Give it *here.*" Before his son, bravado
He presses home the point
and is hard-pressed. Held. Fused.

Flypaper. His teeth buzz
His body curves, shaking, urgent
as a mongrel fucking in the street.

His baby teeth a bracelet,
an ivory oval in the gloom,
little Billy starts to laugh,

helpless, in the grip, oblivious
to the smell of cooking meat:
his father's fingers Tallentyre,

dragged by Jimmy by his jacket
off the mains, still holds the fuse.
"What a bastard " He wags his hand.

"Get the bastard back with sticks "
And so they do. He does.
Without a word of thanks

Like a man about to squeeze
into the needle's squint,
Henry Raine is shrinking,

away from something invisible,
inaudible, a prickle in his blood,
bad smells he now hallucinates

1935:
HOT AIR MAIL

Mutualité, Palais de la, Paris.
Admiration, mutual in.
Russian, idioms for emphasis

in argument, include:
needless to say, to say the least,
and by the way, and in the first place.

Tsvetaeva, Marina Ivanovna,
sexuality of, strong with Sapphic
variations *(see* Parnok, Sophia),

encounters Pasternak, B L.,
transfiguration of, *see* suit,
arranged by Stalin's secretary

erroneously, egregiously
(vide infra inside leg, *supra* sleeves)
amusingly *(see* teeth, tobacco-stained).

For the past, *see* Correspondence,
acrostic in *Lieutenant Schmidt,*
altered archive dedication

to Pasternak of *After Russia:*
"my brother in the fifth season,
sixth sense and fourth dimension."

As for the present tense,
it relaxes in the corridors
of powerlessness, the index

of this international conference
defending culture from the Fascists,
and it collapses into laughter

at his "epileptic" suit,
the stumble in her hem,
burns left by her cigarettes,

confirming Yablonovsky's verdict
on her verse: "she enters literature
in curlers and a dressing gown."

More breathless, gasping laughter,
her hand on his arm, begging,
soulmates in the flesh,

until he takes her by the nose
between the knuckles of his hand,
laughing, leads her to his lips

Corrida in the corridors,
their two bodies flirt,
dancing with the danger of each other.

Observed, complacently, by Efron,
contented cuckold, and Mr B,
eyes and ears of the NKVD,

who are one and the same,
both placid in the knowledge
that, now his hands are full,

Pasternak's preoccupation
with Marinochka and poetry
will reduce the risk of intercourse

with Whites, to say the least.
The whereabouts of Pasternak?
Out of breath. Under her bum.

Or is about to be, thinks Efron,
the snug fit of his (face)
like a flute in its case.

By train from Quai d'Orsay
to Meudon, Clamart by bus,
so Tsvetaeva can pack

her gosling weekend case
for Saint-Gilles-sur-Vie.
Sweeping armfuls like a burglar:

her diaphragm, two flyswats
"useful for beach badminton,"
a shuttlecock like Sitting Bull,

her bathing dress and Efron's suit.
Thus Borya running backwards to the sea,
lest she should spot his spotty back

And the chalet later,
sand-strewn, cold, self-catering,
cognac, conversation, kissing,

then Borya unbuttoned, laughing,
naked, twilit, laughing, lithe,
doing Vaslav Nijinsky in *L'Après-midi*   . .

She will never forget
the squeak of his dancing feet,
ghosts in the ignorant lino.

She will never forget
the one grey hair
she found or what she said

Borya, when you are old,
with an old man's smouldering ears,
there will be fire in your heart

She will never forget
how afterwards she spoke:
what will we do?

And his unforgettable reply
we will forget this happened
Censored. Needless to say

On his return, out of his senses,
he doesn't tell his wife he's back,
proposes to Akhmatova in Leningrad

1935:
WHO WAS BISMARCK?

München: the Danish consul
confers a single, swaddled rose
on every female guest

Outside, it is November,
minus *drei,* newspapers
gathered by an officious wind

Frost deep-fries the ferns
in the Hofgarten walks White
rust. Neglected in their window box,

six suedette chrysanthemums
reproach the consular hothouse
like a model aeroplane:

balsa struts, taut tissue
transparent with dope, unpainted,
grounded, ready for takeoff.

Seeing the thornless rose
in his fiancée's hand, Eliot,
brooding on breeding, thinks:

thorny subject, racial hygiene
(And, observing the innocent cut
of the consular eggcup trousers:

Nothing *there* to sterilise.)
Why, after the United States,
does *Denmark* lead the field?

Why does Germany come third?
Why? Because Several reasons.
Resistance since the law was passed:

appeals clog up the machinery.
That Bavarian Catholic pamphlet.
appeal in *every* case What else?

Doctors dislike notification
relatives of reported patients
take their custom to another practice

Defectives, dipsos, epileptics,
psychos, schizos, deviants, etc.—
all risk being sterilised

should the defect be deemed congenital:
women at a thousand marks,
men between one and two hundred marks

(Prognathous Pouting Petulant
Pin-eyed Pop-eyed Pathological
Tropical fish fan themselves)

Subject to due legal process
before the court *(Erbgesundheitsgericht),*
the case is certified

O.K or not *(erblich belastet),*
depending on the evidence
(der Antrag) assembled

by the district officer for health
E g answers to "elementary" questions:
When is Christmas? Who was Bismarck?

What is the simple interest
on the sum of 300 marks
at three per cent for seven years?

What is truth? Make a sentence
using these three words:
"soldier," "war," "fatherland."

Then, this last October,
marriage laws and marriage loans.
Dwarfs (less than 130 cms.)

not eligible for loans
or tax relief for children.
Jews disqualified as well.

And restricted to specific partners:
full Jews must marry full Jews only;
half Jews must marry full Jews only

Practising half Jews count as full Jews.
Quarter Jews must marry Aryans.
This consulate is full of Jews.

Including Eliot's fiancée,
Lydia Leonidovna Pasternak,
who is dancing to the wireless,

who represents not passion
but scientific principle.
Her "tainted" Jewish blood

is excellent genetic stock.
Besides (he ticks them off),
as daughter of a famous artist

and a former concert pianist,
as sister of a leading poet,
bourgeois breeding with bohemia,

she speaks to Eliot's snobbery.
Social snobbery, not sexual.
His appetites are delicate.

Leonid has painted his portrait
Eyes asleep, brushwork mimed
like the ticking tail

of a cat caught by its prey
And also the sparrow's REM
from sitter to easel to sitter

Refusing Eliot's (agreed) 300 marks
as utterly inadequate:
"Please regard it as a gift."

Or as an obligation.
Look at Lydia now Laughing.
Strong, suntanned features,

somehow slightly masculine.
Her double chin, her heavy nose
Is Eliot anti-Semitic, too?

Laughing like a horse
Flat, unspankable buttocks.
Large aureoles on tiny breasts.

Unlike his gold engagement ring,
she isn't made to measure.
Eliot imagines the ring

next to the red carbolic soap
in the W.C. of the Berlin express,
where he left it—by chance

Why is her body so square?
The innocent cut of his jib,
his lifeless twelve-inch fly

flat as a mangetout.
His "gold" Kensitas coupons watch
reminds him of mortality.

Once more unto the breach.
Youth's a thing will not endure.
He is marrying for children.

And in a week, a week,
to England with his bride-to-be,
leaving behind the institute,

and all the Hitler photographs
hung by brownshirt "scientists"
instead of "Jewish daubs" by Pasternak,

his lab mice whistling like a kettle,
murmuring to Lang in a moving lift,
sitting, in silence, Russian style,

before the journey begins,
with Karlchen on his knee,
with Lenchen astride Lydia,

and everyone crying in silence,
except for Eliot,
Eliot icy with altruism

(that notice at Seeshaupt:
Juden nicht erwünscht)
mired in his own mistake.

1936:
Du Bist wie eine Jüdin

A six-place white bone china setting,
set for Fedya, Zhonya, Karlchen, Lenchen
No guests And no female servants

since the law today forbidding
Aryan girls all jobs in Jewish households.
Lest paterfamilias gets familiar

And Karlchen is inconsolable:
Ilse whom he loves has left,
without a reason. Just goodbye

Because Karlchen and Lenchen
have no idea they are Jews,
that their father, Frederick,

vice-president of the Vereinsbank,
is etc etc Their mother, too
Only Fedya looks as if etc. etc

The plates of lentil soup,
identical, a daisy chain
of Koenigszell Silesian china,

getting cold as Karlchen cries
thick, acid tears, his hot face
constipated with emotion.

She is sixteen, he is six
Hugging her knees in bed,
the patient exposition of her past,

its endless intricate etc etc
and when she lets her earphones down,
she lets him feel her flaxen flex,

and what he feels is love,
"when even if the journey's long
it only takes a minute "

The thought of her teeth,
crooked, white, wet,
the unbroken bow of her eyebrows,

and he is shaken with silent sobs
like the hiccoughs of boats
at their moorings.

It is snowing outside.
rivel–ravel cross-eyed ticker tape
The curtains are open

Then stillness and the soufflé
on the saddle of a bike.
Karlchen crying like a taxi

To cheer him up, the butler, Heinrich,
impersonates a one-man band.
Never known to fail

Each hand shakes a silver tablespoon
stuck in a bottle, while he bangs
the door behind him with his heel,

spraying spittle from his lips
which fart the "tune " A "tune "
Definitely the indefinite article

And when this distraction doesn't work?
Lenchen loses patience with her brother:
Du bist wie eine Jüdin! Scathingly.

Fedya. Zhonya. Karlchen. Heinrich
Silence and the snow's drop-shadow lettering.
Lenchen The buzz of conversation stopped.

1936:

MATTY, THE ACEM GIANT

On the washroom cistern,
a dried sliver of carbolic soap,
crisp as a dental plate.

Cautious, duck-lipped,
Matty's mouth approaches
his coffee. And stops

A tightpuckeredtarpaulinofskin
His fissured finger fishes out
the offence like a used French letter.

Lays it next to the soap
The washbasin, ermine
with oily fingerprints

At least he is able to drink
without using a straw
Matty surveys his damaged face,

freckled in the dusty mirror,
marked and chipped
as the mirror is marked.

How are the mighty fallen,
in the midst of sparring
with that little cunt Raine

Slain in thine high places
Like splinters under the skin,
spelks, his healing cuts

Stitches like false eyelashes
under his eyelashes Left eye
still closed like buttocks,

cleavage the colour of beer.
Shards sharp to his short tongue
No sword in his hand,

the little cunt Raine,
just bare fists at lunch break.
It was Matty's own idea:

"Tell me yerra bit of a boxther
What about a bit of thparrin'?
Put a thyow on for the ladth."

"You're too big for me, Matty "
(True Bigger by more than a foot
Question: how did Raine manage

to mark Matty's face? So much.
Answer: he didn't dare miss.)
"Whath the matter? Are yer yeller?"

And Norman's jacket was off,
jerked to the workshop corner,
one sleeve half inside out:

"Matty, if I was only five stone,
I wouldn't be frightened of you "
The men in the paint shop made a ring,

and in less than ten minutes
Raine made a monkey out of his face.
Now Matty sips at his mug,

turns into the paint shop again,
where Norman is waiting,
a huge wisp of hubris

"Fancy another bit sparring?"
It's an offer Matty cannot refuse
without losing face, but then,

he hasn't much face left to lose.
Putting his coffee carefully down,
for answer, he picks up one-handed

an internal-expanding buffer
and swings its hundredweight of steel
onto a shelf above his head:

"What about a wrethling match inthtead?"
Norman sees the magic carpet of dirt,
the trickle of rust from the shelf,

and nods a silent nod, thinking,
"Serves you right, you silly sod"
and "What the fuck did you say that for?"

The Acem Giant folds him in a hug,
sweeps him off his feet.
Has a crush on him.

Ribs. Impossible to breathe.
Dangling legs. Ventriloquist
and ventriloquist's dummy

So, before he blacks out,
with clenched fists,
Norman clashes both his temples

How the mighty are fallen. Again
Percussion Brain between buffers
Matty is prone on the dribbled floor,

arms outstretched, his biceps
veined, engorged, as breasts
are muscular with milk.

Norman is wearing his work boots
with cast-iron heel cleats.
Teeth clenched, a long jumper,

he jumps both heels at once
into the biceps,
grunting with effort

Bloodless, blue-black cusps appear,
willow pattern, oiled with whey
Norman looks at the useless arms,

hears the noise of his heart
like the clump of a flagstone.
Sits, a mahout on Matty's chest,

the heels of his hands
pushing the giant's chin.
"Give in, Matty "

Matty shakes his head.
"Give in I'll break your neck."
Coarse with pores, the tautened skin,

veins visible like a lizard
under the scarlet skin,
a tent of tendons

"I'll break your bloody neck."
The works' buzzer goes for work,
then stops.

But Norman presses on,
until the Acem Giant gasps,
"Give in, ah give in."

Norman leads him,
like Lazarus back from the dead,
to Mr. Wells Hood, the manager.

Knocks on the glass door.
"Enter " Wells Hood at ease
in front of his stilton fireplace.

Norman beckons Matty forward.
"I want to know who set him on.
And I want a witness, sir

Who set you on to me?"
Silence The Acem Giant's tongue,
a swab on swollen lips.

"Matty, lift your arms."
"Ah can't " "How will you stop me
hitting your face, Matty?"

Pinstripe suit and pinstripe hair,
the horrified Wells Hood protests,
"For God's sake, Raine, please no "

Is overridden by Raine,
whose fist is drawn back:
"I'll count to ten."

The cause is lost in history,
a feud between two men long dead,
their living genealogy of blame

culminates with Norman's curse:
"I hope your arsehole moves
into the middle of your body,

so that every time you shit
you have to get undressed."
It will. In six months' time.

For once, I see ahead
I see the exit wound erupt
Gouged, milled, ground, minced.

Some nobody will pull the trigger,
bullied beyond endurance.
Below the left nipple, a sphincter.

1936:
A BIT OF ABYSSINIA IN BATH

While Jimmy brushes up
the Word of God
(the letter, not the spirit),

Haile Selassie the First,
formerly Ras Tafari Makonnen,
grand-nephew of Menelik the Second,

111th descendant of Solomon
and of Sheba, now Negus,
yea, Negusa Nagast,

Elect of God, yea,
conquering Lion of Judah,
and also, to the locals,

a "little coloured man,"
immaculate in bowler hat,
dark suit and cape,

sovereign of several sticks,
for church, for town,
for inspecting nonexistent troops,

absolute Abyssinian monarch,
subject to severe attacks
of irritable bowel,

is taking a windy, wintry walk
from Fairfield to Bath,
his constitutional,

with Colonel Roniger
three steps behind,
past, first, the cemetery,

past Comfortable Buildings,
past Albion Terrace, past
the Bath Gas, Light & Coke Co.

(owed money by the Emperor)
then past the rusty trio
of turquoise gasometers

(not unlike, thinks Roniger,
the hatboxes from Harrods
flung out of the palace,

with stiff-starched collars
and yards of Liberty prints,
by the rank rank-and-file

of the defeated Ethiopian army,
deserted by its Emperor,
who had taken a train

at Akaki, ten miles from Addis,
crossed the river to Dire Dawa,
and halted in the heat

for several hours in the heat
before crossing the Danakil Desert,
diddley-dum, diddley-dee, into exile,

taking the rheumatic Empress,
her pet papillon puppy,
the silent Crown Prince,

the tearful Duke of Harar,
Prince Sahle Selassie,
the Princess Tananye,

and the Princess Tsahai
to work as a probationer
Great Ormond Street nurse)

until they reach, as usual,
the Ebenezer Chapel,
built in 1910, whose pyramid roof

is covered with quotations
taken from the Holy Bible,
one of which,

                YE

        MUST   BE

    BORN   AGAIN

Jimmy Raine is repainting white,
the one whose sentiment
the Emperor takes to heart

and stares at hours on end,
while Roniger remembers
how the war was lost:

Selassie's Aero-hair
a swarm of flies, heat,
his rows of medal ribbons

like a paintbox, heat,
paying scavengers (with silk shirts,
dollars, satin capes) to skirmish

while the feasting chiefs
drank tej and ate from massobs,
and were demoralised by rain

and by marauding Azebu Galla,
until the Emperor broke off
the war for pilgrimage

to all eleven churches of Lalibala,
each one carved in solid rock,
eating only injera and water,

and afterwards on to Addis
where the war drum of Menelik
was beaten brutally two whole hours

before the Emperor took the train
which took him to the *Enterprise,*
a British cruiser off Jibuti:

all of which Roniger remembers,
watching the Emperor's gaze
glittering like the broken glass

spread by Badoglio's troops,
a kilometre cordon
against the Abyssinian foot,

watching the splosh of white
jump like jism from Jimmy's brush,
waved like a flywhisk at the Emperor,

his complicated pride unbroken
by the bump and grind
of bolts of Liberty prints,

collars scattered like fingernails,
Baldwin's broken promises,
or unpaid gas and electric bills.

1936:

HOLD YOUR HAND OUT,
YOU NAUGHTY BOY

Windowless, high-ceilinged,
the cold, distempered dressing room
has seen it all The one chair,

Co-op cane, over-pliant
The cold radiator The basin,
clean, because there is no plug.

The one metal locker,
chipped beige paint, scarred
tribally with ventilation slats

A scroll of canvas stretcher.
Thin-skinned boxing boots
fainted full-length, taking a dive

And mummified fists,
pot, hard as a lavatory pan
when sweat sets

the plaster of Paris, dusted
into three-inch cotton bandages
before the bout. Like seasoning.

Two hard cases
in two eight-ounce gloves
Punching more than your weight.

And undetectable, unless
the referee not only feels
but also smacks the bandages—

quite hard And not always then.
The boxers keep them clenched
One cough of dust disqualifies.

Later, in the dressing room,
the "spats" are sawn off
with a hacksaw blade

the colours of iodine,
its frayed edge
an edge of bandage, petrified.

The evidence becomes
a bit of builder's rubble
in a Boots Cash Chemist bag

dropped from the train back home
Seeing the saw, Norman decides:
give up the game professionally,

get reinstated amateur Because
Because he is disgusted Morally
Because he was beaten last week

for a shot at the title:
the taste of gumshield
like a rubber johnny in his mouth

Because this dressing room
Because prizes are better than purses
Cases of cutlery Sherry glasses.

A six-place china dinner service.
Because this dressing room
Outside, the evening star

shining like a money spider.
To train by the sea again:
that greyhound's dashed-off signature,

one corner of a cornfield
franked with poppies,
that hare crouched like a moth,

sudden bouts of conducting,
and a tree creeper, there,
tight to the trunk,

see its quick spiral
like a roll of bandage
melting in the second's hand.

1937:
BLACK SHEEP

Late May in the Moscow boulevards:
the chestnut in its convict clothes
and Mandelstam like Lazarus,

returned from Voronezh,
and constantly getting the giggles,
bucked by being back (back!)

after three years in exile.
The process of arrest arrested,
Article 58 behind him at last.

Back! His flat has been faithful:
bare floorboards luxurious,
grained like smoked salmon

under their half-inch permafrost
He wipes a fan of floor clean
with his overcoat sleeve,

frayed cuff freshly trimmed
Spiders sprawl in their hammocks
The radiator hot. Hot for three years!

But his body has gone bad:
along the ripe eyelids,
amber granules of glue,

boils on the back of his neck,
peeled, shining, unplugged,
and the lips composing, composing.

To Borya, gone field-grey himself,
giggling: the menu's changed,
we're in a vegetarian phase.

Once I saw a flock of sheep
being forced into the abattoir.
Their sides were heaving,

but the faces gave nothing away.
I wondered what they looked like
underneath their masks.

Mandelstam, a filthy fledgling,
transparent, lips composing
even as he stops, afraid,

hearing the lift. Giggling.
Fear makes you impotent.
We've said enough to get ten years.

For our wives to stand in a prison queue,
next to the names beginning with *M*
and all the others starting with *P*.

Arsehole puce under the eyes.
Clammy calyx of hair
clagged to his wet skull.

Like the lip of a jug
this bulging Bourbon bottom lip,
composing, decomposing.

1937:

A Room for Roniger

Well-oiled Roniger and Jimm Y
Like a lump of butter
drunk in the frying pan.

Legless Slowly. Dying Henry
Sunk in his shawl, in himself,
in front of the fire

Like a man staring out
at the flight of a bumblebee,
a shrinking semibreve

lost in the loops and threads
of shorthand filling his sight.
Facing the music. Knowing the score.

He cannot be distracted now
He wants to know the answer:
O death, where is thy sting?

He could take precautions.
If he knew. His words slurred
Buzzers a scissors

In the kitchen, Queenie listens,
as Jimmy. Explains. That Roniger.
Just as much a refugee as Lydia.

Who is upstairs, washing her hair
and crying. Soap gets in your eyes.
Choked with limescale,

the shower set speaks
its spider of spray. Cautious.
Long distance. Spindly. Faint.

Eliot hasn't touched her
since their honeymoon.
And then only once in a week.

An icy week at Ilfracombe.
Halfway through he fell asleep.
Or pretended to. Suddenly soft.

Sunrise at 6 by her wristwatch.
Watching the wallpaper,
finding Jewish profiles hidden there,

she heard him masturbating
in the other bed. A whisper
on the linen sheets like breath,

like Henry's breathing now,
careful, almost surreptitious,
trying to suppress the shudder.

What's the difference? In the end?
Italian Fascism. German. Therefore.
Therefore *en-titled* to a room.

Peas keep falling off his forks,
so Jimmy lowers his face. Too close.
The whole weight of his head

crashes into the brisket of beef,
the mash, the peas, the sprouts.
Grounded in gravy, he sleeps.

The law of inertia, says Roniger,
is difficult to judge
Your son, says Roniger, I understand,

has invented the drop-shadow lettering?
Such solemn conversation,
he and Queenie burst out laughing.

Upstairs, Eliot blots his diary:
Father's colon doesn't differentiate
solid waste from gas. Crying

about the butterfly of excrement
blotted into his pyjama bottoms.
Difficulties feeding now.

Swallow reflex nonexistent.
I wish that I could say to him
how much I love him Before he dies

The room for Roniger
will be arranged tomorrow.
He and Jimmy share a bed tonight.

Therefore They turn and touch.
As thick as thieves. Solid spam
Jimmy makes a meal of it. Garlic.

Catching the come in his hand,
the consistency of starch.
Wanking off with it.

1937:
A Prison Visit

In der kleiner Führer,
das Strafgefängnis Plötzensee
where poor Kroll has been detained

is at D2. The end of the tramline.
And then a walk through a wood
with a woodpecker snoring.

Along an edge of canal:
oil like tarnished silver,
burnt Tyrian iodines,

towpath coaldust underfoot,
jet hundreds-and-thousands
like beading on an evening bag.

Leonid contemplates the door,
studded, like a ham with cloves,
and the door within the door.

His gloved finger
on the mint imperial
at first summons silence—

the woodpecker snoring—
then a hawking of keys
and the shutter spat back

Leonid's visiting permit
is plucked from his hand.
The shutter sniffs shut.

The guardroom's great library.
Row on row on row on row of keys,
hung from iron hoops:

sprats, frozen waterfalls,
fighting fans, false Triton beards,
axes, adzes, halberds, hatchets

A coil of quarter-inch rope
as a lighter for cigarettes:
its smouldering chancre

And then poor Kroll,
tearful, still testing the hair
over his bald patch,

one eye like a Victoria plum
Unshaven weak brown bristles
like a kiwi fruit

Beltless, tieless, laceless.
His Latvian passport confiscated
His consultancy with KDW kaput

Convicted of convictions:
part of a solicitors' ring
for getting *Judengeld* out of Germany

And now his son:
tell Sasha to leave for London
Natasha teaches at the Reimann School

(So the son will be safe
with his sister, Leonid thinks,
but what about the wife?) And Zolya?

Unpersuadable. She stays.
We're letting Bayreuthstrasse.
She'll help out at Dambachtal.

Three years. It could be worse
Leonid points to his own eye
and at the question there.

Nothing serious. Another prisoner.
When I wouldn't . . . A pervert type.
I know I look like death.

No, Leonid thinks. Not death.
But cobwebbed with cracks.
And close enough. To tears.

For long. For. Pauses Reflection
Lights gather in the eyes.
Panes brighten and break.

And yet until the time is up,
they carry on a conversation:
Kroll's cell contains a Felix Krull

whose cover is a Catholic priest.
Years ago, he used to do a rabbi.
It died the death with Hitler.

A silk bookmark of hair
flat between Kroll's breasts,
fine as threads on a cob of maize.

1937:

ARRESTED FOR MURDER

Hearing the hinge of the peacock,
Norman, arrested, amazed by the maze.
Of moss, two millimetres high.

The green blueprint of a maze,
and there, at the centre, a bee,
groping stone, like the Minotaur

He hadn't realised the maze was there.
While Olive was shelling canoes,
long ships for lunch, he looked around

Now Mrs Pretty walks towards him
like a buckled wheel. Polio
The click and creak of her brace

Like a bee in her fox-fur wrap,
her polished bun
quilted under its hairnet

"I can see you've found it
You're Olive's friend from Oxford
It's a different make of maze·

always getting lost itself.
We have to weed like anything,
or else it disappears Poof

All the gardeners think it tiresome,
I think Especially Spooner
But it brings my father back "

Spooner? The Romeo she complained about.
Playing pocket billiards
Pointed comments when she rubbed

the Jacobean candlesticks
"Your father?" Norman asks
"Designed the thing before he died.

It's supposed to be a rose
That's why the bee   Did you work it out?"
And Norman: "No. I see it now."

Exhausted what they have to say.
The house in its ivy pullover
Rusty bedsprings of bracken.

Silence. So he volunteers:
"Those cyst things on the heath
should be investigated "

But then the constable arrives
by bicycle from Woodbridge
and takes the winded Norman

into custody: a charge of murder.
A hand on his shoulder,
he turns like someone waking

from the workings of a poem.
Suddenly sees a whole lost world:
that slow worm's stylus,

one eye's pinprick of blood,
and its slow bronze bending,
the ferry's cloak of ripples,

the constable's helmet,
its freeze-dried dust
of rough blue serge,

the badge a monstrance,
and the helmet's dim interior
cathedral light of wintergreen,

two bright bodkins stabbing
through the ventilation holes,
on cracked green linen glaze

the owner's name inscribed
and worn away with sweat to Greek
Eyelets left by feeding fish

The inkpad fills its tin
exactly Curved at the corners
Spongy to touch Cake mix gone corrupt

Press down. Transfer. Press down
And roll Left side Right side
Black frostbitten finger-ends

Then Eliot on the telephone
confirms his brother's alibi
The unnipped nip of handcuffs

A mug of good strong tea,
of tea with poke in it
to perk you up Boxers' tea

He isn't Del Fontaine, thank God,
the French Canadian middleweight,
even though they could be twins.

Whose strangled girlfriend
Double Windsor round her puckered neck
Blue tongue. Squeezed out of its tube.

1937:

THE GOLDEN BOUGH

Two sudden twigs of lightning
The Alps in spats. Gone.
Kidnapped by thunder

The tunnel into Germany
lit by electric sizzle
like a welder's arc.

Then Lydia lets fall
the corner of the blind,
and turns to the compartment:

the nightlight's glow
of bilberries in cream,
sleep, socks, suitcases, sprawl

At 6, SS and customs officers
polite on the threshold:
eyes from photograph to face,

a few pages of passport turned,
returned, a croquet click of heels,
the Hitlergruss and gone.

No "Purpose of visit?" To visit.
No "Why this particular route?"
Better to come to München

from England via Switzerland
because better for a Jew.
A longer route, but less in Germany

From these clapperboard heels,
cut To Fedya's sitting room.
Action. Inaction. Silence.

Zhonya's face has hiccoughs.
Lydia looks at the piano stool,
its four bandy bulldog legs.

Lenchen's new nail scissors
trim off stiff eyelashes
on the doll that Tante brought.

Karlchen arranges Rowntree's Smarties,
a brand-new English sweet.
Quarantined by colour.

The boy has chicken pox:
hard white blobs of candle grease,
windows of translucent fat,

suet crusts, cigarette burns,
craters, one of the damned
in some medieval frieze.

A whited sepulchre of calamine.
Pitted whitewash.
A firing-squad wall.

Fedya, self-made man,
successful banker, Lutheran,
has requested Lydia

to confine her calls on them
until after dark His tense hands.
The anger in his voice. At her.

We have to think of the children.
It's inconsiderate. We love you
But your features look so Jewish.

Middle shot to mantelpiece:
an arachnid Indian goddess
bares her brassy breasts

Juts her butt
Saved from nigger decadence
by the kicking crosses,

swastikas around the base
Dissolve to Lydia.
Her struggling face

The Jewish mouth recites:
One fine day in the middle of the night,
Two dead men got up to fight . . .

The mouth recites:
Frusten war's: der Mond schien helle,
Schnee lag auf der grünen Flur,

Als ein Wagen blitzes schnelle
Langsam um die Ecke fuhr . . .
At least the children laugh

Recites in Russian:
Рано утром вечерком
Поздно на рассвете   . .

Quatsch mit Sosse
Nonsense in any language.
The lightning's genealogies

1937:

ENGLAND VERSUS GERMANY

Gnats flash, dazzle, disappear
on the asphalt outside the Albert Hall.
Then the rain stops. Rough diamonds

The billboard in aspic announces:
England versus Germany.
I am the buzz of anticipation.

I am Pontius Pilate,
procurator, washing my hands
in the whole bloody business.

Box him. Box him. Tie him up.
Legs and feet. Legs and feet.
Left him. Left him Dance and box

I am Pilate, wishing my hands
in the whole bloody business.
Boxing is the noble art

of hitting without being hit.
Just out of reach,
the boxers face each other,

balanced on both feet equally,
the left from 10 to 20 inches
in front of the right.

In the red corner, Otto Kästner,
Olympic champion, oiled, tanned,
hair flighted like an arrow.

His broken-nosed opponent,
Norman Raine: white, visibly veined,
hair wavy as an Alsatian's palate.

Both are featherweights,
the middle of the order
because the English skipper,

a Cockney heavyweight, was scared
begin with the flies
and finish up with the heavies.

But the flies and the bantams
want the fights to be fought
the other way round. Heavies to flies.

So Norman volunteers to start
My lords, ladies and gentlemen,
an alteration to your programme . .

In the red corner,
Marquess of Queensberry rules
In the blue, a caestus.

Which is not a cestus,
an item of ladies' lingerie.
One knocks you down One stands you up.

The classical caestus is a thong
vertebraed with iron balls
like a broad bean

and wound around the fist.
Or sometimes studded with nails
like the husk of a chestnut

Use your reach. Reach. Box him.
Jab. Jab. Feet and jab and.
The left foot is flat,

the right heel slightly raised.
The left side turned a fraction
to present the smallest target.

When the hands are clenched,
the thumb is doubled,
thus avoiding sprain,

behind the third and second fingers
There are several dangerous blows:
to the solar plexus

and its network of nerves,
to the point of the chin,
impairing equilibrium . . .

Foul, ref, foul. Foul
He's using his head. Foul.
Kästner has butted both Norman's eyes

The lids begin to mizzle blood,
split and spirt. A broken fan.
The referee looks at Norman

looking through his eyelids
and is about to stop the fight
and Norman asks for the rest of the round.

Is not refused. Fight on
Eurydamas swallowed his teeth
rather than show he was hurt.

And went on to win
Give him the heel of the glove.
Jamming his left

underneath Kästner's armpit,
Norman pulls his opponent
between his right glove and the ref.

He's holding, ref
And on the blind side,
gives Kästner the heel of the glove,

the lethal trellis of laces
ripped up and down his face
like a credit-card machine

Through a gash darkly,
look at the red on his teeth.
Bright menstrual blood on porcelain

Enough From the back of beyond,
Raine wins on points,
wins by a foul

1938:

The Company Car

One hunchback robin hops Hops
Winds have rinsed the peppered may.
The silence of frontiers.

Sun and the stink of petrol.
A bee like a liquorice allsort.
Wayside flowers waiting to move,

still as a still photograph
As Zhonya's passport photograph
which is causing the problem.

All eyes, taken in Moscow
at the time of the famine,
so starved her periods stopped,

it shows an older woman
than the one crossing her legs,
whsst, whssht, twenty years later,

in the back of this Opel Kadett
like someone posing for a photograph,
leather gloves asleep in her lap

Furious, afraid, Fedya shivers
like water coming to the boil
Zhonya looks straight ahead,

beyond the boom of the customs post,
to where the road evaporates
The horizon's earthquake of heat.

Gestapo boots on the gravel,
as if fuming in acid,
tops accented grave and acute,

grit in the ear
like a faulty connection,
raised seams on the jodhpurs,

black leather glove
holding the passports
A pace behind, the customs officer

in grey with dark green trim
The black buffer hat
bends to the rear side window

Patent peak. Insignia. Brown eyes
"Heil Hitler You can let them through
She *is* Frau Pasternak "

And to Fedya: "Remember me?"
Before the Geheimestaatspolizei,
he used to drive a taxi

"You always gave good tips "
Years ago, when Fedya took taxis,
never the company car and chauffeur,

before this Jewish thing
He wants a lift to Austria
Three on the back seat,

a little squashed,
and Fedya falls asleep
while chauffeur and cabbie

debate the finer points
of bodywork and engine performance.
Better than the 5 8-litre Hansa.

Fedya's head lolls
on the officer's epaulette
Spoke wheels and tiepin bumper

Side indicators fold away
like cutthroat razors.
His glove on Zhonya's knee.

Fedya's mouth amazed in his sleep.
Headlamps behind their mesh.
Zhonya donating her knee.

Swing rear axle.
Independent front suspension.
A buzz eaten by distance.

1939:

Digging for England

Fedya's finger screwing his ring.
Norman digging an air-raid shelter
in the back garden of Garden Square

Sheathing the spade in England
like someone unsheathing a sword.
Or drawing the blackout *Whssht.*

Whssht. And *nggh.* The costive sound
of a soul at stool *Nggh.*
Whssht and *nggh* to a depth

of six feet, a boxing ring
of fifteen feet six inches square.
Sweat leaving his shirt

heavily inked like a lino cut.
Two halves of a worm
squirming away from each other

Fedya's radiant toecap,
studded with opals of dew,
turns out of its nest

an ancient tennis ball,
its sodden pith like a grated lemon.
A snail in its strapless décolletage

The walls are the wooden walls
of the old garden shed
Woozy for years. Easily swayed

Earth steps, down one wall,
finished with apple crate.
The roof topped off with turf.

Overgrown with undergrowth,
four mounds are cleared
on Mrs. Pretty's estate.

Rabbits have left
dun rosaries of droppings.
"Why not start with this one?"

So an approach trench is laid
to the largest by Basil Brown,
the local archaeologist,

on 35 bob per week plus board.
Enthroned in a tub bedroom chair,
a Rose-du-Barry "Lloyd Loom,"

wickerwork frosted with gold,
Brown directs the gardeners,
Spooner and Jacobs,

who skim away the fallen roof
with ordinary coal shovels
on the end of very long handles

like paddles in a pizzeria.
The scabby hilt of a sword,
gold leaf on the wind,

coins like three-quarter moons,
and Phillips called in from Ipswich.
Brown takes a back seat to C W.:

thin hair painted on his scalp
with very broad brushstrokes.
Shovels are set aside

for bodkins and bellows,
the badger-hair toothbrush
At Woodbridge station,

C W. meets the London train
with a tobacco tin
containing a golden buckle,

salted with stones like a pretzel,
and shows it to the BM's Kendrick
on its moist bed of baccy

Therefore the Office of Works
orders a mile of barbed wire,
tying itself in knots

and running around in circles
The *whssht* of the bellows,
the *nggl* of bodkins. For months.

Until: the ship's outline
like a millipede's rictus
left by a wet bicycle tyre

Two apostle spoons
A nest of six silver bowls.
A two-foot ceremonial whetstone

The silver rims and mounts
of seven auroch drinking horns
Wilf Grimes in his boiler suit,

C. W. P. in navy-blue pinstripe,
and Olive in her apron,
packing the treasures in moss,

packing the moss into boxes,
pillboxes, chocolate boxes,
boxes of Meltis New Berry Fruits.

This warrior's moustached mask,
its rust bleeding in the rain,
makes her think of Norman

looking through his eyelids
like someone looking through a mask
She'll marry him. In Oxford.

In Oxford, Zhonya is half an orphan.
Her mother dead of a heart attack.
A new language to learn,

the Anglo-Saxon tongue. *Whssht.*
Sky tadpoles trawling for flies.
War less than a week away.

1940:
Bergen-Belsen

The sound of trains at the railhead
like a saw panting through wood.
Phosphorescent in the dawn,

logs, a stack of birch logs,
loom on the tip of his tongue:
tinned pilchards in translation.

David Kroll, amazingly, smiles.
At roll call yesterday evening,
the Dutch contingent's ragged shout:

Drei Liter. And not *Heil Hitler.*
Straightaway you couldn't be sure
Because it seemed impossible.

Barbed wire like interference,
tearing up the postcard view
Neatly. The German efficiency joke:

some benighted peasant touching nettles,
"Bloody Germans. Electric everywhere "
Probably a Pole. Good for any language

Kroll has acquired a spoon A spoon.
He has already memorised its features.
He would recognise it anywhere.

Now he must find a hiding place
Poe's "Purloined Letter."
Hide it with the other spoons.

Very funny What other spoons?
Think, Kroll, think *Think*.
He will hide it in the same place

it was hidden when he found it.
The owner won't look there again,
once he's looked and found it gone.

Seen it, seen his spoon,
and seen her vanish as he looked.
The infidelity of spoons

And human greed. That poor sod
six months ago, just arrived,
telling his little girl

how everything began: when clothes
were handed out to all the animals,
the monkey and the cat were greedy

and grabbed the first things they saw
Which is why the cat has four socks
and the monkey has two pairs of gloves

Then he had a heart attack.
Unforgettable, his masturbator's mask
Horsey, said the kid, astride his corpse

Father and four-year-old daughter,
matching rings under their eyes.
The colour of paper

about to burst into flames.
What is the reason for that,
the physiological reason?

Zolya could probably say
(His wife, the doctor at Vitel,
a camp for foreign nationals,

less vivid than a spoon,
and quite unable to explain
because the reason is not known

There is no reason to know)
Whereas boiled flies
provide a source of protein

Whereas the starving lie down
because it uses energy to stand
As Kroll does now Battlefield effect

Though when the picket comes
he clambers to his feet at once
The commandant? Why?

The reason is not known.
That margarine paper he stole,
the headache of each lick? The spoon?

You face the commandant's face,
the scar on his cheek like a gill,
those lashless bull-terrier eyes,

crimson with conjunctivitis,
because your daughter has worked,
lobbied MPs, the Swedish ambassador,

paid 50,000 Reichsmark in bribes,
to have you translated to Wülzburg,
another camp for foreign nationals

Here is your railway warrant,
Nansen passport, civilian clothes.
Your daughter remembers you both

by remembering how you dressed
She starts at your shoes
and works up to your faces.

She has an eye for clothes,
she buys for Simpson's, Piccadilly
All night, before tomorrow,

David worries and wonders
whether to save the spoon
or leave it in this factory of breath.

1940:
Ja Bin die Papi's Spoek

Suddenly over your eyes from behind,
Vsevolod Meyerhold's bony hands
and that comic Afrikaans:

Omlet, Omlet, ja bin die Papi's Spoek.
So you always knew it was him
Right shoulder higher than the other,

bow tie, horn-rims, brittle hair,
long upper lip, barrel-stave teeth,
a micro-climate of eau de cologne,

rapid tightrope walker's walk,
and, of course, obsessed by *Hamlet*
He lives in Borya's head,

unprotected, indiscreet, a gas,
describing Chaplin at Versailles,
the grey-haired, suited gravitas

suddenly changing to Charlie,
a minor miracle to please the crowd.
"The classics must live so "

Borya's *Hamlet* at the Writers' Club,
read now by the author,
owes everything to Meyerhold,

onlie begetter and updater,
director not a bloody archaeologist,
dispenser of the proscenium arch

Boris renders Shakespeare's page,
escapes the tyranny of word for word,
takes liberties. Deliberately.

The credo might be Meyerhold's.
Who planned a pair of actors
in the part: one bold,

one indecisive, alternating
in the same performance.
You have to bring the thing to life.

And yet he never did the piece,
but lived up to his jokey epitaph:
Here lies V E Meyerhold, Director,

Who Never Directed *Hamlet* Once
He is dead and gone, lady
And also Zinaida, Wife of the Above,

who was murdered at home,
three weeks after his arrest.
Borya, like everyone, is baffled,

stops in the middle of a line
to wonder what happened,
caesura sliding into silence

Sliding into total silence.
Put you out of your misery?
I was there on both occasions.

Protesting Buzzing the actors.
Naturally enough. I'm bloody-minded.
No question, I can be bloody-minded

What happened was this
bio-mechanics at the Lubyanka,
a limited range of gestures

They began by breaking his spectacles
and he began to be scared.
After this oddly effective first act,

they broke his left hand
It was rather a scream.
The bare minimum of dialogue

Unwilling suspension of disbelief
Spotlit, a ghost without his specs,
vague, pale as distemper,

except for the definite umlaut
red on his nose,
he signed the document, V E. Meyerhold

It took him almost two hours,
his signature's electroencephalograph
Left-handed. Apart from anything else

He implicated everyone
He implicated everyone
In triplicated everyone

And she? The wife? Zinaida Raikh?
They put her eyes out, first.
She only answered the door,

as it happened, to no one she knew
They pressed the bell continuously
Who's there? They pressed the bell

It was ten past 3 in the morning.
And then she thought she heard
Ja bin die Papi's Spoek.

It was hard to tell
She drew the bolts, top and bottom.
Four total strangers stood outside,

one a woman, pressing the bell.
She couldn't see their faces.
"We come from Vsevolod Emilyevich."

Cheka. "Won't you please come in?"
Actress, she turned in her kimono,
buttocks slowly chewing the cud,

and never reached the drawing room.
Fingers over her eyes Pressing the bell.
She could feel his cock grow hard

Gat-toothed, Borya stands aghast,
adrift, alone on the bare stage.
And is saved by Tsvetayeva,

arrested in the doorway, late,
without Efron, without Ariadna,
grey, ghastly, ghostly, all alone.

Borya leaves the stage,
takes her hand and kisses it,
leads her to a front-row seat

1940:
VARIOUS PRESERVATIVES

Pale cherries bottled in blood,
an igloo of eggs, upside down
in isinglass, submarine plums,

kitchen windows crossed out
with Union Jacks of sticky tape,
sandbags sheltering against the walls,

and Rudi Mendelssohn, the father,
with Rudi Mendelssohn, the son,
sitting in the basement kitchen

where the daughter used to work
Newly shipped from Germany
under the Panamanian flag

From Dachau to Harwich to Oxford,
via Nürnberg, Würzburg, Aschaffenburg,
Frankfurt, Osnabrück, Emden,

to attend the inquest in Putney
and identify her frozen corpse
A kept woman Waiting for weeks

Her nose was broken off
like a classical statue
She was furry with frost,

looked blind from both eyes
Lydia asks about Dachau
There are two camps, not one

Induction and the main camp
The first a disinfection station:
they take away your clothes,

supply fumigated camp pyjamas,
clipper off all body hair,
inject against typhus,

one needle per 50 inmates.
In the main camp everyone works,
but everybody wants to go there.

Why? He rubs his bristly head.
The lavatories are clean
Washrooms too. Headed Dachau notepaper

Now he asks about Erna.
Impossible to tell the truth.
Couldn't trust her with children.

Lydia offers an egg instead
Bruised pastel plush yolk.
Says: I found her difficult.

She stuck hats with hatpins
on my father's portrait paintings.
Made mistakes in her English:

getting down to brass taps.
Lydia can't translate the joke.
We got on badly. She left for London

Mendelssohn tells the table-top:
she went to Mrs. Brookes's bedroom
naked one night. *Gar nichts.*

She tried to get into bed
Twice. Both sides. In total silence.
One side, then the other No

She lay down on the floorboards
Five minutes Dressed Disappeared
Next day, dinner at the Dorchester,

then jumped off Putney Bridge.
The railway bridge. A ringweight,
20 pound, tied round her neck

He looks at Lydia now And laughs
For us, it is lucky A lucky escape
Two fingers shoot his temple

Knock-kneed ungainly ghost
Caught against the curtain
Body hair: spiders round each nipple

Her groin, her armpits:
the black blaze of dead fires,
dark holocausts of hair

1940:
CHRISTMAS DAY IN BED

Eliot and Jeanie have been playing
doctors and nurses most of the night
in Will and Mary Sargant's empty flat.

After Chaplin as *The Great Dictator*,
Adenoid Hynkel, the secret Jew,
Dr Raine and staff nurse Fyfe

walked back through the blackout
towards their theoretical desire
and the Sargants' Siamese cat

with its oiled black ears
like the tips of chicory
left in walnut oil. Pre-war.

Her high heels prattled,
answered to his weightier brogues,
flirted with falling in step.

Eliot would prefer to eat her pussy,
would like to pull it apart
and get at the guava, juices

tart on the tip of his tongue.
He would like to tell her this,
wallowing in "cunt," the word.

Instead, a longish walk to Bayswater,
discussing Chaplin's didactic strain
and its diametric opposite,

the suddenly terpsichorean tyrant,
whose balletic grace and balance
are meant to show the opposite,

a crank, the balance of whose mind
You almost wonder what side he's on
Silence Talking of which.

The balance, Eliot means
Drawing on his briar, Dr Raine,
confides, aposiopetically,

a case, history, of, interest,
to, a colleague A corporal in the RAF
Demented after Dunkirk. Mania

Obsessed with abbreviations
BEF, e g Or DPM, camouflage,
Disruptive Pattern Marking

Anyway (Why, thinks Eliot,
rationing his phrases,
weighing his words, professional,

arranging the stem of his pipe,
this amorous austerity?
I want your *Liebensraum*)

The fucking British army
beat him fucking senseless
in some fucking sand dunes

they were fucking sheltering in,
because their fucking regiment,
or what was fucking left of it,

came under fucking friendly fire
from a fucking Spitfire,
and the fucking cry went up:

the R A fucking F The R A fucking F
You fucking little sod
You little sodding fucker

The RAF in strafe The marram
flattened like flame under a saucepan
Low. A flying Singer sewing machine

firing a double seam of shells.
In stitches. The CSM's teeth
all over his face Pissing himself

Fists for hours on end And belts
The corporal's face soft fruit.
Spoiled fruit. Torn fruit Jam

At night he finds it hard to sleep,
feeling the force field again:
foreshortened, furious features

crammed up against his own
And so he needed morphine,
broke into the poison cupboard,

took between five and seven grains,
and survived unscathed Unscathed.
He woke up in the morning

Eliot brains his briar on his brogue
and feels for the key. At last,
the Sargants' basement flat,

where it isn't worth lighting a fire
Cocoa substitute? *Camp?* Tea?
(Tea ration forethoughtfully to hand.)

They keep their coats on,
smile at the kettle like a patient,
and chat about the Kaiser,

still alive, at Scheveningen,
watching the North Sea mixing cement,
in his invalid carriage,

legs in the black rubber sheath
like a merman, talons on the T-bar,
turning his back to the Nazi invasion

We should be in each other's arms,
instead of talking all this tripe,
thinks Eliot Beauty on the bed.

On a pillow, Sargant's note,
superscribed to Eliot Raine, Esquire,
in steel-nibbed copperplate,

already fading blue-black flourishes:
Pray feed the animal.
Provender within the meat safe

Mithras be with you
Enjoy a happy Saturnalia.
To't, Luxury, pell-mell. Will

How can they enjoy themselves
in front of all this furniture,
the upright audience

of dining room chairs,
the buttoned-up sofa
on its best behaviour,

knickknacks and props
in some Victorian period piece?
Acting the part,

they brush their teeth,
wash in cold water,
taking turns in the bathroom.

Paired in pyjamas,
they crawl between cold sheets.
Passionless peppermint breath.

His fingers on her breast
shocking as a stethoscope
The only human touch

a groaning, intermittent ghost
somewhere in his bowel's oubliette
He rubs her right hip

like a radiator, risks
a gynaecological caress.
Squeaky intercourse concludes

with coitus interruptus.
Then folded like a frozen fly
But in the middle of the night   . .

All the same, all the same,
leaving Jean, he feels the same
as leaving Lydia A huge relief.

1941:

MAWCARSE

Let me try to put you in the picture.
Action painting What a bally mess
How best to piece things together?

We could start with a definition
How do you define a Scotsman?
A Geordie with his brains bashed out

We could search for the dead
by the light of our cigarettes
One of the injured is smoking a fag

but something is seriously wrong
He exhales smoke from everywhere
except his mouth, like a Turkish bath

Love moans come from the wounded
The whole of his battledress top
is oozing fog like a freezer.

I should explain where we are.
Mawcarse is an RAF bomb dump
in a guarded pine wood.

Smashed, it smells of disinfectant
Bunting, bits of battledress,
branches fluttering with flesh

Peaceful as a Shinto shrine
Where were we now?
Between Kinross and Milnathort

I could say who I am·
that trickling sensation,
which might be blood. Or sweat

Or tears. Or something else.
Last night, tonight, was Hogmanay,
and the squad got wrecked.

Legless. Bombed. Out of their skulls.
Which is why Norman looks pissed,
soused enough to be singing,

O tell me the truth, mother,
tell me the truth,
do kippers swim folded or flat?

Cross-eyed, unable to focus,
black tongue, fuddled feet,
tomorrow he'll be on a fizzer

They'll charge him with malingering,
with bloody Munchausen's, because
he isn't bleeding from the ears

He has a triple-fractured skull,
internal bleeding, and, in days,
acute subserous meningitis

He's awa in the heid Wandering.
Down by the stream Birdsong.
All the willows washing their hair

The perfect plumage of pine cones
A threadbare spider's web Fucked.
Big black cock in his kisser

Oot on it   Completely fucked
In 28 days, he'll forget the lot
falling out of the jeep,

two field hospital operations,
let alone his letter to Olive
from sick quarters in camp

"Head injured by a piece of coal "
His handwriting   Signed it "Geordie "
He hasn't the faintest idea

1941:

PROFESSOR DOT

A blackbird chiselling granite.
Dawn at the Edinburgh Royal
Norman is lying awake,

the wince of sound in his ears,
his shaven head on the pillow,
seamed like a hot-cross bun

He is thinking things through,
Professor Dot's latest prognosis.
Yesterday morning The big chief,

talking to Dr. Watt,
toying with a book of matches
like a Red Indian headdress.

As Norman raised two knuckles
to rap backhanded on the open door,
he heard dispassionate discussion

What are Raine's actual chances,
now he has had the first fit?
His hand, double-stopped, in mid-air

like a fiddler's fingering. Wait.
Eighteen months at the very outside.
As little as that? How will he go?

Without knocking, Norman interrupts:
Good question How *will* I go?
Professor Dot is displeased.

The cube of ash on his cigar
is contemplated and brushed off
Perfect coordination.

Not eavesdropping, are we? he asks,
lugging his left leg on its pedestal
as he crosses to close the door.

Every step he takes
like a clockwork cowboy
trying to mount. On his high horse

Norman: I was going to knock
But the door was wide open
Silent, these rubber-soled

And Dot: Well, you may as well know.
I diagnose a slow deterioration
in the brain's left hemisphere

Your right side will get paralysed
Then I'd predict a rapid decline
Blindness Possible madness Death.

Eighteen months As I said
Tell me, what do you remember, Raine?
Give us some idea Anything at all?

The runway at RAF Leuchars
like a squash court with skids
Landing lights in a line

like pins in a tailor's lapel.
To det 4,000 pounders,
you needed three tapes up.

Fully detted bombs
had detonators nose and tail
and all along their length.

Sunk in sponge rubber Prophylactic.
Anything could bring them off.
Winched straight into the bomb bays

When you sawed the top off my skull,
the pressure I felt. Not pain.
The pong of burning bone

The hesitant, crumbling buzz
of surgical brace and bit Stopping
Hardly anything at all, he says.

1941:

THE GORBALS

Norman and Robert McGregor:
A C Plonks, the only two
recuperating at Gleneagles Hotel

All the rest are officers
Longest way up,
shortest way down Quick march.

Give the saluting a rest, old thing
Red-eyed in the rhododendrons
Weepy with stress By the dozen.

Which means the airmen
get a bathroom to themselves.
Other Ranks, for the ablutions of

The cold tap's icicle,
the hot tap's dry uncontrollable cough.
A caddy of toothbrushes

But McGregor brushes his teeth
by lighting a fag,
washes by combing his hair

with water out of the hot
Yet, perfect teeth, white,
and odourless armpits

McGregor, in front of the mirror,
expelling a fart with a frown
Get out and walk. Severe.

Norman feels his new hair
for the holes in his skull.
A shamrock of inners. Another.

They are going to Glasgow,
to McGregor's home in the Gorbals,
on a weekend pass, in hospital blues.

But his new address
has somehow gone into hiding.
He has to ask where he lives,

where the house-warming is
Door to door, like detectives.
Whisht Dinna say that. O K ?

In the stone tenement hallway,
a dark continent of urine
and the McGregor coat of arms:

a long cock and balls,
in chalk, like a DDT spray
Now he minds where it is.

Mrs. McGregor bursts into tears.
Or bursts out laughing. Or both.
She has taken a drop. Aye, a drop taken.

After the Gleneagles Hotel,
the glaze of T'ang vases
(dusky duplicates sunk

in rosewood surfaces),
Persian rugs on parquet floors,
dimpled Chesterfield sofas,

this limbo of smoke,
of uncarpeted concrete
Mrs McGregor is sick in the sink.

Like a beer pump Twice.
Burps Lights up a nip Exhales
Feela bit billiards.

The seatless, waterless WC
is set over a cesspit outside,
down two stone flights

The T'ang of ammonia
from an underworld of excrement
The bottomless pit

Furry with grey fly,
the porcelain bowl, stirring.
Like a shaven armpit

Diz Norman wanni diman ring?
Fo fefteen boab? Wonni thes?
Solitaire clasped like a cauliflower

They're not hot, are they?
Dinner be sane that O K.?
Everyone's listening Everyone

So bring over Benny Lynch,
his yarmulka of baldness,
Tolstoy's thermometer nose

Annitha wannyi boaxas, Benny
(Ex-flyweight champion of the world,
bobbing and weaving,

punch drunk or plain drunk,
broke as his nose:
longest way up, shortest way down)

Wass sure nem, Jimmy?
Norman Raine Knobser Raine
Herder ewe Herder ewe Bias her drink

And in the *Mirror* on Monday:
GLASGOW JEWELLER MURDERED
Dinner breathe a wurd. O K ?

Or yirra ded man. Snow joke
Yi can haud awa till Egypt,
disguise sell find use Terra.

Nigh forra nigh Justice
How do you plead? Human
For mercy, forgiveness.

Norman is flaming well guilty
Her name is Elaine
and she works in the kitchens

Her joke about Hughie McEwan:
garbled Gorbals for Menuhin
It was innocent, perfect,

till she brought him round
after 15 three-minute fits,
touched off by Technicolor

when they went to the pictures
An arsehole of lipstick
blotted on Bronco. Pictures.

He hasn't seen Olive since Christmas
Eight months Where does he live?
Red-eyed in the rhododendrons Both

1941:
FIRE-WATCHING

Bombers above and the braille of stars
Twelve storeys down, the dusty street,
blind in the blackout.

A humid September night, searchlights,
dutiful Boris out on the tiles,
in shirtsleeves, armband, soup plate

At the far end of Lavrushensky,
an apartment block eviscerates,
hit by four or five incendiaries

Sturm und Drang Coup de foudre.
Twisting its galvanised windows,
breaking china, breaking glass,

tearing itself apart, baring
its soul, on fire like Hercules
Or like Tsvetayeva in love

Who was the torch she carried,
who taught poetry the torch song
Her Joan of Arc "the pyre is mine

Theirs the transcript of the trial "
Filing clerk and firebrand,
setting fire to herself,

always surviving this art of scars.
Until something was broken down
The transcript of her trials?

Call Boris Leonidovich Pasternak.
Buzz. Buzz. Silence in court.
How does the witness plead?

Guilty Guilty before God
(Boris has found out from Fedin
about her suicide in Elabuga)

She told me when we said goodbye
at Khimki River port
that she was looking for a hook

and had been looking for a year,
since her return to Russia,
paraffin, dishwater, and paranoia.

Sunshine squiggled on the water
I felt that she was talking for effect
It sounded written. Something for a poem

I told her to look for food instead.
They had nothing for the journey.
She thought the boat would have a buffet

One suitcase full of loose cigarettes.
We can always smoke for breakfast
She bought two open sandwiches

and waved her silver bangles
Goodbye. They shone like irons
I saw the wash. It came and kissed

the wharf and travelled on.
I felt relieved to watch the boat
go round the bend Low in the water

She was dangerous to know
and hard to help. Still arrogant,
after three months in a cupboard,

sleeping on a trunk We sat
on Peredelkino Station platform,
talking poetry, rhyme schemes, scansion,

ignoring all the trains to Moscow
She, oblivious And I?
I was frightened she would miss the last

Zina wouldn't have her in the house.
Now she lodges in my conscience,
still taking five days

to polish up some hack translation,
twenty lines of poetry
I'd knock off in a morning.

She couldn't compromise
I begged her not to go to Elabuga
but was glad when she went

to save her son from bomb disposal.
The worthless Mur. His bitten nails,
the taint of gouda on his fingers.

Telling her how old she looked.
True. When she smiled, her teeth
were like an X-ray of teeth.

A deep, dirty, circular seam
ran right under her chin
from nostril wing to nostril wing,

like a ventriloquist's dummy.
The skin was orange peel.
Under the eyebrows, unironed.

Caught without her spectacles,
she shied away from books,
held literature at arm's length.

Skin tags like tonsils, milts.
Ankle socks Her knitted beret
like the halo on a toffee apple

Thin, but thick in the waist
The puckered cleavage
Still she bore herself

as if she were a beauty
Cream cheese impasto
with radishes and gherkins, chopped

Her last words to Borya were:
I am already dead Have been for months
One cassata sandwich Want a bite?

Exactly twenty-one days later,
Tsvetayeva had found the hook
and hanged herself Not because

she had failed to get a job
as dishwasher in the writers' canteen
(Too many other applicants)

Because, in Chistopol, three people,
Misha and Tania Schneider,
Lydia Chukovskaya, had taken pity

It was a touch of warmth
in which she burned alive,
A Woman Killed with Kindness.

Wood, thinks fire-watching Borya,
solid, reliable, and suicidal.
Ruins chainsmoke like Tsvetayeva.

1941:

BLITZ

Haunted by *Blithe Spirit* still,
thinking of Jeanie's thorn-shaped navel,
her russet pubic goatee, the Blitz,

and Lydia's discovery of his diaries,
Eliot peers into the blackout
over his Hillman's steering wheel.

Though better than the two inch hole
and single stem of light
laid down in earlier regulations

(a waste of wartime cardboard),
the single headlamp's brief bouquet
is glaringly inadequate

And streets keep disappearing.
You turn right or left into rubble
Trial and error. Cliffhanger Street.

You need to be clairvoyant.
Sometimes you are clairvoyant
and see, *plein air,* a porcelain hippo,

ascending into heaven,
the mixer tap's top brass
and its trachea of braid.

Or a first-floor drawing room
like a raft tilting over a waterfall,
poised with furniture

and perfect with Persian rugs
Pity about the incontinent pipes
Shame the fireplace shat itself

And now the sirens start
like Munch's woodcut of *Der Schrei*
(82 degenerate works seized in 1937).

When the windscreen shatters,
Eliot pulls over to the curb,
and says they should enjoy the show.

So shitstruck he forgets
the cowering helmet under his seat.
He thinks of Regensburg,

and a fountain's faint ghost,
naked, bruised by a rainbow
But the shock of the bombs

brings him the shock in Lydia's voice.
Why am I poked? Why am I poked?
Eliot could hear the Singer

tapping its foot, somewhere upstairs.
And then full blast: I asked you
a question Why am I poked?

It says so here "Poked L." Thanks
(Not this current year, thank God)
Why are your other ones "rogered"?

Why can't I be rogered or trevored?
Lydia's tearful attempt at a joke
like the wailing All-Clear.

Eliot covers his eyes,
discovers wet on his cheek
Superficial cut to his scalp,

requiring a couple of stitches,
3,000 units of ATS by injection,
so over London Bridge to Guy's

Where Eliot is known But not Lydia
So everyone assumes that Jeanie .
Very nice to meet you, Mrs Raine

No contradiction No going back
Bombarded by greetings, by light
Outside, night dark as chocolate

In the dispensary office,
Izzard explains Wittgenstein:
famous philosopher from Cambridge

that no-one has heard of,
hiding behind an alias here,
job as dispensary porter,

there, with the arachnoid eyebrows,
arrogant sod, excuse my French,
tried to show me how the unit should run

(Plunges the needle into the phial)
And he won't let the other chaps whistle
I cannot tolerate these musical mistakes,

it is too painful; kindly stop Egotist
He can whistle a bloody Brandenburg,
Beethoven's Pastoral, Schubert's Unfinished

(The hypodermic's premature ejaculate.)
That should do the job O.K.
And you Bye-bye Take care Take care

Back in the car, Eliot dons his helmet.
Doesn't even offer it to Jeanie
Drops her at the Nurses' Home

1941:

CHISTOPOL

Outside, minus 30 Twice today,
annunciations Leafleted by snow
Puddles cracked like cranefly wings.

Inside the writers' cafeteria,
Brrrrya's talcum breath,
his English-Russian dictionary,

his *Romeo and Juliet,*
his woollen, fingerless gloves,
the numb, fingerless fingers,

and what Akhmatova now designates
"the almost unbelievable luxury"
of granulated sugar in a bowl

(true, the bowl is missing a chip
and complete with brown bogey)
A recent refugee from Leningrad,

she remembers going to a shop,
an expensive place by the Hermitage,
to buy in for the siege,

six days before the Germans came
Too late, of course, but six days
felt two years away. Oddly relaxed.

Borya observes her heavy breathing,
the sudden snag of her thread,
the way her needle picks

at the huddled spider.
No flour, no salt, no bread
They had caviar and almonds.

Which she therefore bought.
And ate before the blockade began.
Then starved And starved.

Until (eyes searching the ceiling,
voice arrested, hand to mouth)
she ate the prison parcels

set aside for forwarding to Lev,
via the window at Kresty,
on the Vyborg side of Leningrad.

To God knows where. Glazed with tears
(Lev Nikolayevich, the son,
who was once her child,

green bruises on his shins
like a new potato.
My God, just think, thinks Borya,

a new potato. A new potato.)
Tactfully, he turns to Shakespeare,
"to remove that siege of grief from her "

A tang of tango from the kitchens.
Deep, silent road outside.
The double windows dim,

shuttered tight with snow.
He finds his place. Back to IV Sc i.
"Or shut me nightly in a charnel house "

The doctors were butchers,
a source of suspect salami
Night soil was disposed of hot

before it froze to bronze,
needing to be chiselled free
Borya studies his new *valenki*.

White felt Unusual and elegant
He has heard all this before.
Needle-eyed at her needle eye,

Anna Arkadyevna Gorenko
squints, rethreads, begins again:
she lay in bed all day

and fantasised foam baths,
scented, hot and rustling
From which she rose, a poodle

Borya would like to change the record.
He opens the door to the kitchen—
for warmth, for the noise,

for a glimpse of women dancing,
breast to sloping breast Appetite.
Feeling feeds his fingertips.

What did she think of Kostya
doing Gorky's Nizhny Novgorod twang,
his "borrowed likeness of shrunk death"?

1942:

TREMBLING

A temple to Mithras
discovered by bombing in London;
items of seventeenth-century armour,

salades, taces, tassets, sollerets,
discovered in the River Ray
from the Battle of Islip;

and Norman in hospital blues,
on Dover tablets
and using two sticks

to walk from Garden Square
up to St. Hugh's, a patient
under Professor Hugh Cairns.

The college is requisitioned:
a hospital for injuries of the head.
Do not ask him how he is.

He will start to tremble.
His lower lip will start to tremble
Where it feels for support,

his left hand will tremble
in the potpourri of paint
flaked onto the windowsill.

Blackouts more often these days.
One side of his head is shaven.
A dressing of paraffin gauze

protects his skull and scalp
from the chafe of his airman's hat
They have put in a silver plate

Shudders like the buck of sperm
And stops Eliot has seen him
but failed to explain it to Olive

Attractive girl, by the bye
His study of occupational therapy
takes St Hugh's as a test case.

Should be occupational therapies
Rickman is administrative head
and hated by all the housemen

When he comes into the common room,
they inspect their shoes for shit,
they drown his conversation

by turning up the wireless set.
Last week, a general came to lunch
When Rickman filled his glass,

twenty housemen at the table
passed their glasses down as well
Nice enough chap But no control

When he turns the wireless down,
they gather round the set
and use their stethoscopes

Decidedly attractive girl
A good pair of tits
when she suckles her son.

White and gold in Garden Square,
Mrs. Pearson's papal flag
celebrates each Allied conquest.

Brotherly love. Stitches like flies.
And the moon like Tom Rakewell
out of his baldy in Bedlam

1942:

ARRESTING IKE

In charge of Torch, of Gymnast,
of Bolero-Roundup-Gymnast,
of everything from soup to nuts,

General Dwight D. Eisenhower,
so kiss his stern, O K ?,
you surly Scottish so-and-so's

Tunnel time is 9:00 P M ,
Gib time is 8:00, an hour earlier,
and Jimmy Raine is guarding the rock

He has shaved his moustache,
tired of being teased
for looking like Hitler.

A low pyramid of pallor
on his upper lip One stripe up,
4th Battalion Black Watch,

an outfit in disgrace,
posted to Gib as a punishment
because they cut and ran,

funk and disorderly,
instead of a strategic retreat
to the dunes of Dunkirk

All day, sunlight has divided
like cells on the sea, and gone.
The full Mediterranean moon

is brighter than a microscope.
Still in civvies for security,
in case his plane was downed,

said to be in Washington,
Ike has been to pat the apes,
for luck, with Captain Butcher,

and Private Kronke, his driver.
South of the old Moorish wall,
the lavatorial lope

of the famous Barbary apes,
limbs like lianas,
showing their tonsured rumps,

cushions of callus,
vulvas like strangled inner tube.
Cracking fleas

in teeth like bitten fingernails.
When: who the fuck goes there?
Jimmy Raine on sentry go, seeing

some jerk in a jerkin and chinos.
And then two more in the dusk
So he looses a round over their heads,

and the supreme commander
surrenders like a Morris man,
waving two white hankies aloft

So scared, I could've fucked his arse,
says Jimmy later, in the mess.
Aye, I knew it was Donald Duck,

but I wanted the arrest to be logged
First, the guardroom's regatta of glass,
and then the regiment's deepest regret Aye

1943:
OREL

One of six with a military mission,
Boris is filling his notebook
on Turgenev's Spasskoye estate

buds tight in puttees,
trout breathe like tweezers,
a squirrel shudders up a pine.

Tines of sunlight through the trees,
where Ivanov and Azarch
are looking for mushrooms,

downcast, with folded arms
and wet, inquisitive toecaps
So. A giant puffball, solid,

slick with dew, resilient,
texture like touching a dolphin
Delicious. Already Simonov

is fixing a wigwam of fire
Lard Salt Unfold the frying pan
And look A lizard like bellows.

The zip of its tongue
taking a gnat and a gnat
from the dodgem of gnats

The waiting Dodge will take them
back to the front at Orel,
but first they will eat,

and Borya will walk on tiptoe,
crucified, up to his waist
in the black, icy river

Then he'll slide in stocking feet
from room to room to room
across the woven, wooden floors,

while Serafimovich laughs
at the literary sacrilege,
throwing back his big, bald head,

the polished tan of a pomegranate
Woooh! and another *niente* ending
The length of the semicircular building

This is the life. Woooh! Woooh!
Whereas Orel
A corpse like a chorister,

eyes filled with dirt,
ack-ack like valerian drops
in a glass of water,

artillery raising a row of poplars,
garbled houses, cardboard coffins,
or that funnel-shaped ditch

where the dead were packed
like a barrel of herrings
The lowest welded by weight

The ground buckled by gas.
Rippled with stench. Borya prefers
this moth with brazier eyes,

frogspawn's filthy ermine,
its sexual slime to heavy transports
cutting Cyrillic into the fields.

1943:
TRAM

The nervous, dusty doors of the tram
open and slap shut like an umbrella,
admitting Borya and Gladkov,

who take the two steep steps,
gripping the steel stangs Hup
Opaque windows like greaseproof paper

Full All the wooden aertex seats
are taken Standing room only
Smells like a kitchen, of sweat

Cigarettes crushed flat, Turkish,
greasepaints on the cleated floor.
Every armpit a sodden salt mine

An old woman opens her bag
for a bottle of smelling salts
Clears her head Pickled diamonds

While they corner, Gladkov whispers
he has recently heard from his brother
Boris's latest book received

Drift lost in the railing of rails
Deliberately Because they don't exist,
it is dangerous to discuss the camps.

The gamboge tram corrects itself
Jolting Indignant metal. Roils
Righting approximate cubist curves

Borya waits for the row to subside.
Then, at the top of his voice:
your brother in the camp at Kolyma?

To think of Anton reading my stuff.
(An acrid asterisk of bluebottle,
the frazzle of overhead poles.)

I have another friend, he says,
who has an ironed handkerchief.
When things get bad, he looks at it.

The clean weave keeps him sane
Civilisation. When you live in a latrine   . .
Everyone is listening Everyone

But what power has poetry against . .   ?
Borya leaves his question levitating.
Against the permafrost, he thinks.

Against the grind, the beach like liver,
against the black mosquito storms,
against the heaps of seaweed,

for use as fertiliser, effervescent,
stinking of stale sex,
stacked by connoisseurs of poetry.

His talking has emptied the tram
but continues to the terminus.
Borya, dead and buried,

like a clam's powder compact,
open, sandy, mirrorless.
Rescued by the terrified turntable.

1944:
MY POOR FOOL

What became of Walde? Walde?
Poor Walde. Asked to plead,
at first he couldn't speak,

hair suddenly seeded with sweat
where it thinned at the temples
His knee trembled in one trouser leg

(How now! A rat? Up a drainpipe,
according to the WPC,
the one who made the arrest)

His lips were sealed,
by a thin red line
of rubber solution,

stickily blackening, blackening.
The pool of wrinkles
deepened on his forehead

as he fought to speak, to speak,
to speak the unspeakable Guilty.
Walde had said he was innocent

(well, not guilty as charged;
what he did do was bad enough)
but the case had brought on his shingles

He had been tight on the tube,
playing footsie and egged on
by the smiling woman opposite

Or: from Chalk Farm to Hampstead,
hiding behind his attaché case,
the accused took out his penis

and masturbated in full view
Mlud? In my full view,
shielded from the other passengers.

I could see the accused was circumcised
At Hampstead, we took the lift,
and the accused was given in charge

to a uniformed constable there
(Waiting. Conveniently loitering
hard by the conveniences)

The character witness for Walde
was Dr. Eliot Raine, psychiatrist.
Has known Herr Walde seven years

Jewish refugee. Gifted teacher.
First offence Court appearance
perhaps sufficient punishment

Momentary aberration. Post at risk.
Fined £15. £4 down.
Seven days to find the rest.

So, outside, Eliot signed a cheque,
postdated, for eleven quid.
Pity you're not a pederast, Walde:

flies to your wanton boys, eh?
Much better bet Cheer up, Walde.
It's not the end of the world.

And they wrangled (sotto voce)
in Lyons about *Lady Chatterley*,
Eliot's only contraband copy

which Walde had not returned.
Except that he had. And, for him,
it was the end of the world

One night, taking a cut
through the university parks,
Norman walked into Walde's shoes

Ouch. Head to toe Pure coincidence
A left and a right upstairs
Knock knockout. Who's there?

A pair of semi-brogues,
clicking their heels,
cooling their tan willow heels,

belonging to Walde,
chin on his chest,
looking askance, black looks,

looking down his nose at Norman.
At the end of his tether
Highly strung.

All of which Eliot recalls
when he discovers his mouth is dry
and *Le Doctorat Impromptu*

has disappeared from his desk
But for a bit of fluff,
the deed box is bare

Panic and emptiness.
His tongue, his cheeks, are suede.
His heart bumps and grinds.

Fear fetches up the perfect excuse:
part of his professional work
on sado-masochism Psychopathology.

Spanking Colonic irrigation Bondage
This, though, will scarcely explain
Eliot's own original stories,

six, pornographic, handwritten,
which have also been swiped
They could be copies Invent authors.

Were they signed? Or unsigned? Shit.
Crucial and he cannot remember.
Why did he leave it unlocked?

Might as well have cut his throat.
And then the General, poor sod,
returns from twenty years ago.

I am dying, idiot, dying.
Eliot was leaning with Norman
out of the first-floor window,

like yachtsmen, so they could see
into the summerhouse next door,
which belonged to the General.

A single pane
that wasn't frosted glass
showed a trunkful of erotica.

We stole the lot:
Illustrierte Sittengeschichte
von Eduard Fuchs, with artistic etchings

of "Das Klystier," "Das Strumpfband,"
"Ohne Scham" by Félicien Rops;
The Culture of the Nude in China,

with 32 original photographs
taken by Heinz von Perckhammer.
Perckhammer Fuchs Nice names they have

And every last airbrushed etc
We were scared to death
Thank God he didn't die. Not then.

Eliot's unpublished article,
"On the Physiology of Spanking,"
is already writing itself.

Just as the tumescent clitoris
fattens on platelets like a pulse,
so, in the secondary sexual site,

blood and supplementary stimulation
are brought to the epidermis itself
Rosy-fingered porn. The perfect alibi

1945:

LEARNING TO BREATHE

Outside, it is raining
On the road, sparks of rain,
then rain doing a rain dance.

Ski sticks, deck tennis, quoits
on the pond at Peredelkino.
Through sliding glass,

the garden wavers, bleeds, runs,
a waterfall of falling greens.
Inside, Boris is watching

the way the body breathes.
With difficulty. With concentration.
Totally taken with the task.

The intercostal muscles
manage to part the ribs,
so the rib cage is lifted, up,

for a second, and dropped again.
He sees for the first time
how heavy the weight of it is.

It stirs The diaphragm tautens,
trembles, and takes the strain,
so the air pressure drops

To make good the loss,
to right the fault,
air is drawn down the trachea

and into the thorax
Because Adik is dying at twenty
of his tubercular spine,

he has taught his stepfather this.
that breathing isn't a blessing
but a state of continual crisis.

Instability Imbalance Emergency
Air pressures needing correction
The rib cage and the heart

are not allowed to rest
Otherwise he is perfectly still
Adik lies on the bed like a lizard.

All wiring and spare parts,
on his side, like a kit,
to Borya he is still a little boy,

sent to sanatoria since the age of 11
and getting steadily worse.
Always too busy for Borya,

now he is busy with breathing
The air is chapping his lips
Brittle, cracked like a prawn,

but he doesn't complain,
until he suddenly cries out
at the pain in his leg

Amputated two years ago.
At the top of his thigh,
soapsmooth uncircumcised stump.

Then the buzz of breathing stops.
Adik has seen something
somewhere a long way off

After the illegal cremation
(Adik's last wish, fixed by Fadeyev),
Zina will bury her first-born

under the flowering currant
by the dripping dacha steps
in the harp of the rain.

1946:
REUNION

Still stencilled with swastikas,
front wheel casings like spats,
peristaltic, single prop,

a Focke-Wulf 190 at Luton
shimmies in the shock of heat,
waiting for Natasha Kroll:

priority flight to Paris,
arranged by Simpson's. Purpose:
fashions for the Christmas windows

(And meeting her mother,
missed for almost ten years)
Perfume and petrol

in the cockpit's blister
The joke of being a Jew
in a German warplane Laughter

Petite A touch of Tartar
in her sloping olive stone eyes
The mapping-pen exactness

of her eyebrows' Indian ink
Features cleverly asymmetric
Skin fine as Rizla papers

She is wearing a Simpson's suit:
five-button, neat grey check
And an overcoat with astrakhan trim,

curly as walnut, slightly waisted,
gold glass rosebud buttons
Her dark red hat is on her lap

so headphones can be worn
and the pilot proposition her
with dinner, dancing, drinking,

with offers to explain
in detail the etymologies
of jazz and joystick.

Offers she cannot refuse
because her mike-switch is kaput
Headphones in her lap,

two bakelite bluebottles,
intermittent, indecent, over
and out, she thinks of England:

of hydrangeas in Hyde Park,
subtle shades of litmus,
of helter-skelter whelks at Brighton,

of taking her parents to Lord's,
of a cricket ball in wet outfield
like a circular saw,

of anything English *Novy mir.*
Aus der neuen Welt.
And when she holds her mother tight,

the fierce love she feels
exists with irritation. As of old.
Love has broken a rosebud button.

1947:

NOVY MIR

The good offices of *Novy Mir*
and Olga Vsevolodna Ivinskaya
bring out the poet in Pasternak:

a peacock's train of typing keys,
manuscript like mushroom gills,
chandeliers, pewter with dust,

like giant jelly moulds.
An affair with words.
Twenty years between them,

and separated by six feet now:
Borya in Ivinskaya's bed,
wearing jacket, waistcoat, shirt,

tie, vest and woollen underpants,
while the experienced Olga,
widowed twice at 39,

puts a crease in his trousers,
which are sopping wet
from a night on the streets

He is here to break it off
Bed preserves his modesty
8:00 A.M She is in her dressing gown

Unmoved, he sees her body move
The shift and sway of flesh
he shrinks from Cold Old.

On the wireless, the fly duet
from Offenbach. *Orpheus.*
Which she switches off

as her dressing gown opens
and she gets into the bed,
giving him a good long look

at the cleft of her cunt
Its ragged shadow
complicated like a Yale lock

Novy mir. Without a hair.
He has only to touch it.
And he has forgotten the cyst

on the side of his skull,
pricked with pores,
disgraceful dandelion head.

Afterwards, he is born again
She sits on the edge of the bed,
belly a coiled anaconda.

He grins with damp-stained teeth
and pulls off his clothes.
Her last husband, she says,

made love like someone sawing logs.
In out, in out.
The second time, she comes herself,

lost, farting with her cunt,
face turned away,
fist-fucked like a French horn

1948:

MYSTICAL DELUSIONAL EXPERIENCE

Rafts, radiators,
panpipes of icicles,
an organ loft of icicles,

and her son's right leg
perfectly paralysed, too,
tight to the bone

as a descant recorder
It matches the useless arm
hanging like a broken pointer.

Spring at Winterton Hospital
The path to Outpatients
and Outpatient Physiotherapy

sunk deep in the snow,
hard, uneven, treacherous,
melted, refrozen,

like a length of dried snot.
The boy's gabardine shoulders
work as he walks.

Whimpering leather.
The snick of stainless steel
Bright as sealing wax,

the leg in its brace.
This rude mechanical,
strenuous, double-jointed.

Like cranking a car.
Effort. Resistance and give.
A rocking-horse action.

Completely different
from cases of cerebral palsy,
tottering like marionettes.

Winterton oppresses Olive.
When the fever was critical,
she watched all day,

on tiptoe, calves aching,
through the observation glass
of the isolation ward

for infantile paralysis.
His glazed features
found and lost with fatigue.

Profile clear as a cameo,
then gone. It was two days
before she could turn her head.

Now, behind his spectacles,
the eyes of the physio throb.
A gaze coming and going.

He powders the leg with talc
and lightly rubs: careful
not to tire the little limb

Or himself. Medical horse manure
Norman knows he can heal the boy.
By massage with linmethsal

Features palsied with contempt,
his index finger prods the air,
intimidates the oxygen

(Like Lenin a long way back)
His hands conduct his conversation.
He has had all the proof he needs.

(Probably 80 proof, says Eliot)
Last Sunday, he went back to bed
in his clothes, after his paper round

And was galvanised Taken Possessed
By Massa, a Negro guide
He said the Lord's Prayer

and called on Massa by name *Massa*
Whuff Norman eyes his audience
Defies his audience to disagree

I was big as Battling Siki.
My head hurt from the headboard
There were weals on my thighs

where the footboard dug in.
I worked the measurements out
I was six feet seven tall

Blood on the boil.
An unbearable light
And afterwards, his neck   .

(Pain in the neck, says Eliot
Either a touch of meningitis,
or an epileptic fit

with mild schizoid psychosis.
Thus Eliot Raine M D., F.R.C.P., D P M ,
the accredited shrink.)

But the son is cured.
Freddy Gargett an encore.
The left calf muscle grows,

a new development section,
its tone improves,
hardens, relaxes, dynamic

under Norman's virtuoso fingering,
while he sings out of tune
spiritual after Negro spiritual.

1949:

BEDLAM

A satisfactory Maudsley morning
coir-coloured squirrels
flame up the wych-elms,

laurel hedges glitter,
the fountain is a firework,
and the star of Bethlehem

(or Bedlam) is focused
in the curve of a Bentley boot,
the long and short of it,

a golden printer's carat
Morning rounds over,
Eliot settles to Sherlock Holmes:

"The Empty House" and Moriarty,
"motionless as a spider
in the centre of his web "

When the telephone rings
The empty warehouse acoustic
announces a butcher who what?

Could you repeat that, please?
Who wants his daughter's kidneys back
Like chestnuts in pith,

ripped untimely,
for sectioning and preservation
Bright's Standard P M procedure

When her body was returned,
he opened it Professional interest
To see what the doctors had done

Eliot can see him, bloodless,
open-mouthed, red-handed,
in his smoking cold room

Bare window two packets of Paxo,
a sprig of plastic parsley
on a willow-pattern plate,

and a sign saying CLOSED
The fume of breath
around his livid lips

Now he wants her kidneys back,
back in her burgled body
Eliot: the Napoleon of crime

Chap in Ward 6 who *was* Napoleon
Haemorrhoid case from St Mark's,
successively reincarnate,

whose presence is marked
by a light behind his head
whenever he goes to sleep,

and his advent heralded
by signs in the night-time sky
Celibate scion of God,

and woe to any woman
he should lie with,
damning her to certain death.

God's scientific expertise
botany, physics, thermodynamics
Laws at play around His throne

60   Innocent as his set of dentures.
Except for the sunshine effect
at the head of his bed

Which disappears instantly
when Sister wakes him up
Staff call him Bright Boy

Pale blue eyes Belfast accent
Forehead furrowed genealogically.
Parting the pitted grey of zinc

Says everything twice
Says everything twice
Hearty double handshake, like Hitler

This very moment in Garden Square,
Queenie watches her husband Henry,
wearing pyjamas, whistling,

take the cold kettle
and fill a hot-water bottle for bed.
Broad daylight. As if she weren't there

1950:
MISSING THE BOAT

Zhonya, abandoned in Boulogne,
missing boat after boat
because of that Saturday's storm.

Rain like a cow pissing
and Fedya simply furious.
Her legs wouldn't go up the gangplank.

They counted the luggage,
sat, and set off for the sailing,
but the steamer forced itself

against the granite jetty
Perverted, hysterical steel.
And Fedya left on his own.

The storm emptied a teapot
the length of the coastline.
Yachts like Hassids in the harbour

Left to her own devices,
every morning, for a fortnight now,
she cultivates her calm,

drinking coffee in the same café.
Zen. She pays attention to particulars
The line of drips left on the cup

sometimes makes a book of matches
Her lipstick sometimes leaves
a segment of blood orange

on her glass of orange juice
She cares about coincidence,
things coming together.

Her single, solitary once.   .
Beauty behind her at last,
she likes watching the waiter,

a boy with a notch in his nose,
new every morning,
from squeezing a spot.

Now he pulls a palsied face
at the counter's chrome
to corner a pimple

close to his mouth
Routine eternal recurrence
As if she weren't there

So she could stay here forever,
phoning Lydia twice a day,
after every missed sailing.

Meshuggah ist Trumpf,
she shouts into the telephone
Remember your children, Lydia replies

Yes Her children as children,
diving for Mr Husband
down to the foot of the bed:

a warm hot-water bottle,
or a cold flabby fool.
Hard to tell the difference Alas

Impossible to extricate oneself.
Every rock pool is flypaper
in the lightly falling rain.

1951:

YAM YAR

Johnnie Frost. Railings webbed,
decorated with dusty nets
like English Italian restaurants.

World gone grey overnight, what?
Distinguished, silver, in sunlight.
Then suddenly drab Like Wodehouse,

curious cove that Lydia's reading,
where several sentences
of puce Quintilian euphues,

prose of the purest penthouse,
are swiftly succeeded
by a plunge to the basement,

my giddy aunt. (Who heard Hitler,
asked if he spoke French, reply:
vous êtes mon prisonnier. M.G.A.)

Jeeves Takes Charge
is bivouacked on the kitchen table,
where Jeeves judges Nietzsche

to be "fundamentally unsound."
(Odd verdict for a Vichy type)
Lydia looks as if she's seen a ghost

Which, in the circs, she has.
Ernst Rosenfeld, wag, Untermensch,
and old Swan vesta from Munich,

who's survived the whole bally show.
Thanks to Ilse, his Aryan wife,
who kept him well hidden

Not even their kid knew he was there.
For five years. Old Chinese proverb:
the squeaky wheel gets oiled

Gestapo aiming their oil cans
like churchwarden pipes
Ghastly. What could a blighter do?

Under the floorboards? Why not?
Rather. Right through the war
Suited her down to the ground

High-minded female, my wife.
Kept me out of trouble. O.S V.s
Trouble is, she understands me.

A year for his bedsores to heal.
Between suspended floor and ceiling
not a lot of room for movement

Awake all day in the dark.
No naps. Too dangerous to snore
Disciplined excretion: nights only,

when no one else could smell.
On a willow-pattern plate.
The dread of diarrhoea

Five years fearing appendicitis;
difficult, though, to catch a cold.
Ration cards for one adult

and one child: food was short
and it was awkward drinking
lying down, hard to tilt

Warm enough in winter,
but hideously hot in summer
Toothache only happened once:

worked loose by hand
then twisted out Painful
And very tiring for the fingers

It was like being quadriplegic:
he kept "clean" with a flannel,
but failed to fall for Nurse

Lisa is sitting on his lap
Aged six. Hearing a bedspring
of wind. She wants a story read aloud

To her he is a total stranger,
so she is like his little girl
Lydia looks Offended. Tender.

Loving. Frosty. Like his wife.
Lisa is lost in *William,*
his way of saying Yam Yar

1954:

CASE DISMISSED

Alfred Bowes-Lyon, the accused
Occupation: steel shearer,
on guillotine at Morris Cowley.

Middle-aged, weepy Alf Bowes,
facing the scars on her face,
raised scarlet seams,

sewn like sample cricket balls.
Hit for sixes. And sevens.
But it isn't cricket

The charge: attempted murder
Defended by his barrister brother,
the Rt. Hon Thomas Bowes-Lyon.

Exhibit A: the big, blunt axe,
snatched off the coalhouse floor
Intent, therefore, impossible to prove.

Curved hickory handle,
bell-skirted head, 3 lbs weight.
The edge's clean, clipped fingernail.

The defendant was jealous:
she had been to a whist drive
The assault took place

in the vestibule of Smeddle Street.
The weapon somewhat unwieldy,
the space confined,

constrained by coats,
a murder charge avoided.
Several glancing blows

before the head came off
The axe, not Mrs Bowes.
(Laughter in court)

There were no witnesses
The neighbours at number 22,
Norman and Olive Raine,

were listening to their wireless set
Light Programme. Derby Day
A successful each-way bet

on a 33-to-1 outsider,
the American mount of L Piggott,
the unfancied Never Say Die

Neighbours at number 18
were on holiday at Minehead
Call Eliot Raine, psychiatrist

accused is not "McNaughton mad "
Clearly, Bowes did not believe
that Mrs. Bowes was firewood

Yet Bowes not legally responsible
Eliot cites case histories,
frequent family mental trouble

Nerissa Jane Irene Bowes-Lyon,
confined to Royal Earlswood,
Redhill, Surrey, since 1929

(There, but not all there
Alive and kicking and screaming,
though "d. unm Feb 1940,"

according to *Burke's Peerage*
Fenella Bowes-Lyon, the mother,
"failed to fill out forms completely.")

Related to the royal family.
Cousin to the Queen. Tingled web.
Mingled yarn The case stitched up

Bowes bound over for 18 months
And what really happened?
He opened his shoulders

Olive adjusted the volume
to screen out the screams.
Hysteria for the final furlong.

Opened the battering
Top edge. Meat of the bat
Snicks, sweeps, hooks, cuts

Blood is thicker than water.
Almost as thick as paint.
The lino treacherous as trout

Dorothy Bowes's cuntstruck face.
Cubist with clefts.
Pitiful prognathous wounds.

There will be scars In time
A quilted, muscular collage
Blue-black permanent. In time

1955:

RADIATION SICKNESS

When your body is afraid,
as Shura's body is afraid,
it is no use saying

there is nothing to be afraid of.
The body shouts you down:
you have no saliva left,

your elbows and your upper arms
have succumbed to eczema,
granules the colour of Lucozade.

There is a keen, magenta,
in each corner of your mouth,
and confectioner's custard

pale in one tear duct.
Why is he wanted
at the Ministry of War?

His summons is the carbon copy
typed on grey official paper:
dry grass and splinters

frozen in dirty water.
Every letter has its aura,
every stamp its afterimage.

Signed with a set of initials,
an indecipherable spider
Shura has a week to worry,

to wish he had important friends,
and *now,* not Mayakovsky
fifteen million years ago.

The clod in trousers,
out to shock the bourgeoisie.
The crowd in trousers,

acting up the demagogue.
Hard to get him off the phone:
yes, I know your Rolls is waiting,

so I won't be very long;
I'll be five more minutes,
then I'll take questions

for, say, ten minutes more,
then you can toddle off, O.K.?
Volodya. The myth of Mayakovsky.

A cloud in trousers. Maya.
You never knew where you were.
Whereas now you go to the guichet

at Entrance E and take a ticket.
Which is read by a woman in wellingtons.
You follow her torch

down a set of stone stairs,
along an unlit corridor
to a door with a leather wedge.

A. L. Pasternak? In 1940,
you were posted to the Caspian Sea.
Where you filled in this form.

Shura's handwriting, held
by a corner, as if contaminated.
He has forgotten this form.

Which declares two relatives abroad:
your parents Leonid and Rosalia
And Rosalia Like someone deaf,

Shura mouths the words he hears
I have two sisters also abroad
We know you have We know you have

Date and initial all corrections.
Towards him, upside down, the form
Now you may go. May go.

The pen, comrade. The pen
In the boulevard's sub-zero dust,
Shura, bloodshot on a broken bench

The face has gone already.
Only the mouth remains
Working Equivocal. In close-up

A couple are kissing beside him,
the man's hand inside her coat
A starling's quiet Geiger counter

1959:

RONIGER DIES

Vell. The Cowley Road Hospital
Anatomical hands on the blanket.
Chin dipped in desiccated coconut.

Mr. Roniger can only say Well,
Sister says to Lydia. Vell. Vell
Here lies the exoskeleton of Roniger

Brown veins on the back of his hands.
Brown varnished vulcanised gums
like pretzels. Folded fingernails

(Unfolded fingernails?) He used to say
he was as old as his tongue
and twenty years older than his teeth.

Sheets thin as a ladies' handkerchief.
You can see to the mattress ticking
and outside there is sleet,

a neat layer like tracing paper.
Able to hide less and less.
The thinnest disguises Vell.

Asked in the past about his past,
he wondered why Angrily.
Why does anyone want to know?

Source of income: secret
He could afford to rent the room
and hang about the Union.

One soft leatherette suitcase,
velvet with dust, under the bed
at Garden Square Not even locked

Containing pornographic magazines
(Spick and *Span* and *Spanking Monthly)*
as well as a letter from Einstein,

in German, and a cornered spider
Here, on his hospital locker,
a pleated, half-peeled clementine

Still life. Vell Last words
I never liked you when we were alive
Sleet a Rosetta stone where birds have been

1960:

FALSE TEETH

Every flowerbed a bed of nails.
Borya's old bath in the nude,
an odalisque holding her pose.

And Ivinskaya kept in the dark,
jealously watching the window
where Borya is dying downstairs,

wedged upright with pillows,
a wax maquette without false teeth.
And serve him right

for Renate, she thinks
For the way he looked at her,
the way she laughed

with her crinkly nose,
wet teeth, wet eyes. Wet furrow.
Kipper bone of pubic hair

The way she kept holding his hand,
their interlocked fingers.
Her parted lips   Wet fern

Ivinskaya can see the television,
Zina's, its four-inch screen
a shiny pellet of chewing gum,

a coathanger's kiss curl,
and Borya's tragic *moue*
more of a coathanger than ever

A cushion of sunflower seeds
sustains her: a fly's eye,
eaten like embroidery.

She is forbidden the dacha,
politely, by Shura and Zhenya
So Zina will not be offended?

In case the emotion is too much?
Because they took his teeth away?
His vanity? The reasons change.

(But, were you to ask me,
I'd say she was too demanding.
Marriage Marriage And marriage.

Am I wringing or rubbing my hands?
A bit of both Whetting my wings
Think of all that foreign currency)

She waylays Marfa, the nurse,
and discovers they've diagnosed cancer.
Both lungs Will they operate?

Marfa's hand on her raincoat arm:
when you open up cancer
it blows all over like feathers

He'll be gone by the morning.
In fact, he is already deceased
Shura and Zhenya,

brother and son, are busy now
putting letters to death,
letters demanding recognition

and still alive with consequence.
Like hair after death.
Like fingernails. Foreign false teeth.

1966:
MOUTH MUSIC

Spertamozoon worming its way
into his Fauvist left ear,
midwinter maroon,

metal teeth of his cardigan zip
catching the cold afternoon sun,
Jimmy is walking to Padarise

along the Edinburgh-London line,
in his pinstripe suit
Who does he think he is?

Rasumov? Evelyn Waugh,
ear tundish offered to guests?
Ramusov? Beethoven?

He is making mouth music.
Sometime last month, a shout
came to live in his mouth

Limping like a skateboarder
because his legs won't stretch
from sleeper to sleeper,

Enid is on his one-track mind.
1915–1955 She Sleeps with the Angels
Cancer Black blood in her cunt.

Ened, Hebrew for *delight*.
Iron cliché, the signpost says:
Enidburgh, 120 miles

Which is where she lives,
in the Garden of Ened
He pictures it clearly,

a sliver, nothing much,
between two railway lines,
the Gritis and Euphrates:

a pond like mint sauce,
collection plates in the tree,
a hawthorn hedge with crockery

The turntable a spider's web,
six several lines,
all leading somewhere . .

His bottom-set stuck out
for comic effect
like a ventriloquist's dummy,

Norman enjoys *Jackanory*,
watching it through binoculars,
when Olive brings in the *Mail*:

Oxford Man Found Wanking
On Edinburgh-London Line.
Our Jimmy. All is forgiven. For now.

Even the fate of Norman's scrapbook.
Whose cover shows two dogs,
torn from scraps of paper,

scrapping. And is empty.
"Fame" filched by Jimmy
for the bar of his pub

Lost, the only record Norman had
Posters, cuttings, photographs
of cocky conquests, gumshield out,

ready to be taken by his corner.
Ten years ago? Twelve years ago?
Can I borrow your scrapbook?

Brought it back empty. Posterity
Now Norman records his voice
A yard and a half of spools.

Of "Spanish Eyes." Of mouth music.
Tone deaf. Not stone deaf
But Jimmy, not Norman, is nuts.

1971:

Constance

Zhenya's big black umbrella
weeping from its widow's peaks
Seed after seed after seed.

Now it stands in a map of grief
next to the plywood door
in this two-room flat

on the outskirts of Moscow
Zhenya, Alyona, Lisa, Li:
listening, a frieze of elbows

on the tiny kitchen table
To Nadya. Nadezhda Mandelstam
Her full mahogany mouth,

the baccy breath,
the hennaed upper lip,
amber stumps in iron settings,

the *café crème* velvet tongue
harshly pronouncing sentences
Laying down the law

Li's doctorate on Shakespeare?
King John is the bard's best play
Because The character of Constance:

grief fills the room up
of my something child,
my absent child,

lies in his bed etc etc
Recites then have I reason
to be fond of grief And nods

Her second book, the sequel,
is ready in the next-door room
More dynamite in there

A new lease of life for M
She lights another Laika
from the previous stub

A Dutch fog, she boasts
What my translator tells
Because it never clears

The Pasternaks have brought
an offering of pussy willow,
a big bunch from Peredelkino,

heavy, silky soft, seductive,
like the brush of the sable,
the carnivorous Siberian sable

She burns the branch ends.
Lights the gas stove
and thrusts them in the flame

To make them last
It is a conscious gesture,
something to be quoted

She isn't intimate
the way she was ten years ago,
a guest at Peredelkino,

redcurrants from the garden
in her lap, not saying much,
snatching flies,

an old woman in a smock
and dark blue kerchief,
hair in a tidy dumpling,

ten years before,
before the mouth of split mahogany
was broken by words,

the seizure in the grain,
this ripple in her table-top
of combed wet hair,

two shades of gold,
her guests bear witness to
Before this metamorphosis.

1974:

University Challenge

Drills *fzz*. Eating a scone,
on the edge of a sofa,
Maria Vladimirovna Romanovna,

heir to the Russian throne,
first cousin of the Queen,
freshman student at LMH,

about to fail prelims
a second time in PPE
Wrrrugh! The drill cuts out

We exhaust the weather
All that blueblooded begetting,
all that DNA, to bring Victoria,

alive, eighteen, and unamused,
to a first-floor rented flat
above a dental partnership

1977:

IRONY INTERNATIONAL

A chemical pelt of hoarfrost
thick on the garden wall
The iron gate sticky with cold

Ectoplasm in every mouth.
Scurf, scales, dandruff, silicates,
minerals, diamonds in Benenson's collar

as he leads the way to the barn
where the bonds have been bagged.
Baler twine like fuses fuming.

A cockerel retches in the rafters,
flares up, tarnishes, fades.
It depends on the light.

Russian railway bonds, tobacco bonds,
North Caspian Oil Exploration.
Worth a million pounds on paper.

Roughly. The rouble equivalent.
They want a tenner to take it away.
A present from Peter's grandfather,

the rascal on the Russian side
who made machines to polish rice
and lost the lot in 1917.

The long drought of history:
dried and broken paint like lichen
all over the St Petersburg palace

Every year he fucked a ballerina.
The kiss-off was a sapphire brooch.
Fresh feels and partners new

One of them threw vitriol.
His face looked like that cockerel.
Lost one ear Rather hot stuff

Dribs and drabs like Jackson Pollock
Needed a new quarter-face.
The family still pay her off

(In 1986, at Sotheby's,
Mussolini's death certificate
will go for £2,640

and Albert Einstein's passport,
the Swiss passport, for £4,180
James Joyce's death mask

will be withdrawn from sale)
Across the early morning dusk,
we see a sudden butterfly

tearing itself in two And again.
These bonds are worthless.
Frozen assets (Till autumn 1986)

1982:

History Repeats Itself

General Eisenhower (all royalties
to the Incorporated Sailors',
Soldiers' and Airmen's Help Society):

London and Abilene,
sisters under the skin.
Swords into ploughshares.

Ike impromptu, on the balcony
of Mansion House, to the crowd:
I am now a Londoner myself.

And JFK to the ditto
at Schöneberg City Hall:
Ich bin ein Berliner.

Impromptu from phonetic prompts:
Ish bin ein Bearleener
still an echo in the archives.

Norman was vaccinated, she says,
with a gramophone needle.
Here to serve our apprenticeship.

When I came out of the forces,
crocked, if I'd known *then*
what I know *now*, what these hands,

I'd never have put on a boxing glove.
(Swords into ploughshares.)
Out of the forces, crocked.

(I am a *zzzzz* on the armchair,
dead to the world,
while his healing hands

make a masturbatory click, click,
like a gramophone record come
to its end, its end, its end.)

1984:
GEMÄLDEGALERIE, DAHLEM

The electric train am Zoo
like a dead fly on its back:
Craig and Lisa descend

with two Chinese inventors
and their triple-tied luggage:
the acupuncturist is S. J. Wu,

whose business card
gives his adderss in Taiwau;
the puncturist is Jenq Maw Lin Jang,

whose new self-sealing tyre
incorporates a "casing structrue"
that stops the air from "leaking ont "

Two pair caterpillar eyebrow.
Two pair standard tadpole eye.
Good luck Goodbye Taiwanese twius

In the Gemäldegalerie,
Holbein's merchant seals a letter,
his neck silk faintly frayed

and perfectly painted,
goose quill packed with polystyrene
In the foreground of the van der Goes,

a single ribbon of straw, creased,
exactly seen and set down
on the canvas: impure gold.

Bruegel's *Blue Mantle* is under glass
It illustrates proverbial sayings
and was painted 1559, the year

he changed his name from Brueghel
Where two pair buttocks
loom out from a lean-to loo,

a mass of fingerprints,
exactly seen, set down
Sie scheissen beide durch dasselbe Loch

Which means they are close friends
In *Predigt Johannes des Täufers*,
a woman in the foreground dusk

is caught by Rembrandt
holding her little girl trussed
so she can shit in the river

Craig pulls the door marked *Drücken*
Wrong *Drücken* was the word
that Zhonya used to Fedya,

feeble when he went auf's Klo
And Lisa's passport holds
her father's photograph,

Eliot taken on his deathbed
Foreshortened face Eyes shut
Chin tied tight with a sheet

Mouth open at each corner
like the symbol for infinity
Straining to relieve himself

And the sign for a wheelchair
is exactly like an ampersand.
An ampersand. An ampersand